1 MONTH OF
FREE
READING

at
www.ForgottenBooks.com

By purchasing this book you are eligible for one month membership to ForgottenBooks.com, giving you unlimited access to our entire collection of over 700,000 titles via our web site and mobile apps.

To claim your free month visit:
www.forgottenbooks.com/free312650

ISBN 978-0-428-69671-9
PIBN 10312650

VISCOUNT DUNDEE :

FAMOUS SCOTS SERIES

~~SC UN~~
~~D NDEE~~

BY
LOUIS
A : BARBÉ

FAMOUS
·SCOTS·
·SERIES·

PUBLISHED BY
OLIPHANT ANDERSON
& FERRIER·EDINBVRGH
AND LONDON

The designs and ornaments of this volume are by Mr Joseph Brown, **and** the printing is from the press of Messrs Turnbull & Spears, Edinburgh.

To

MY SONS

LOUIS AND ADRIEN

CONTENTS

CHAPTER I

CONTENTS

CHAPTER VII

CHAPTER VIII

CHAPTER IX

VISCOUNT DUNDEE

I

FAMILY, BIRTH AND EARLY LIFE

THE Grahams of Claverhouse were a younger branch of an old and illustrious family which, from the twelfth century onwards, bore an important part in Scottish affairs, and of which several members figured prominently in the history of the nation prior to the time when the fame of the house was raised to its highest point by the ' Great Marquis,' the ill-fated Montrose.

The Claverhouse offshoot was connected with the main stock through Sir Robert Graham of Strathcarron, son of Sir William Graham of Kincardine by his second wife, the Princess Mary, daughter of King Robert III. During the early years of the sixteenth century, John Graham of Balargus, third in descent from Sir William, acquired the lands of Claverhouse, in Forfarshire, a few miles north of Dundee. From these his son took the territorial title which, a few generations later, was to become so feared and so hated throughout covenanting Scotland, and which, even at the present day, after the lapse of more than two hundred years, is still a bye-word and a shaking of the head to many.

John Graham, the 'Bloody Claverhouse' of Whig denunciators, and the 'Bonnie Dundee' of Jacobite apologists, was the son of William Graham of Claverhouse and Lady Magdalene Carnegie, fifth and youngest daughter of John, first Earl of Northesk. On the authority of Charles Kirkpatrick Sharpe and of Mark Napier, successive writers have stated that the mother of the future Viscount was Lady Jean Carnegie. Sir William Fraser has pointed out, however, that Lady Jean was only his maternal aunt, and that she married, not a Claverhouse, but the Master of Spynie.

This mistake as to the name of the mother of Viscount Dundee, adds the author of the 'History of the Carnegies,' is the more remarkable that she bore the same Christian name and surname as her cousin, Lady Magdalene Carnegie, first Marchioness of Montrose.

The precise date of Claverhouse's birth is not known. Biographers, accepting Napier's computation, almost unanimously assume that it took place about 1643. That is based on an erroneous deduction from a note to a decision of the Court of Session, quoted by Fountainhall under date of the 21st of July 1687. The matter under litigation was a claim put forward by Fotheringham of Powrie to levy fish from the boats passing by Broughty Castle. The Lords decided that his charter gave him sufficient right and title 'if so be he had possessed forty years by virtue of that title.' With special reference to one of the three defendants, it was added, 'as for Clavers, he was seventeen years of these forty a minor, and so they must prove forty years before that.' Napier assuming the seventeen years of Claverhouse's minority to have been coincident with the first seventeen of the forty referred to, argued that, as a period of forty years prior to 1687 leads back to 1647, Claverhouse was not twenty-one years of age until seventeen years after 1647; in other words, that he was of age about the year 1664, and, consequently, born about 1643. The calculation is ingenious, and the result plausible; but the marriage contract of Claverhouse's parents proves the fallacy of the original assumption from which everything depends. That authoritative document, for the discovery of which we are indebted to Sir William Fraser, was subscribed in 1645; and the objection which that raises to the date worked out by Napier is obviously insurmountable.

For the approximation thus shown to be erroneous, the 'Dictionary of National Biography' substitutes another which has the merit of being more in accord with the known dates of some of the events in Claverhouse's career. A memorandum preserved at Ethie and noted in the 'History of the Carnegies,' supplies the scrap of positive evidence upon which it is founded. It shows that, in 1653, Lady Claverhouse, as tutrix-testamentar to her son, signed a deed relating to a disposition which she was bound to make to two of her kinsmen. It is not improbable that this was done shortly after her husband's death. If such were the case, their eldest son, who, according to the note to the decision of the Court of Session, was a minor for the space of seventeen years, would have been four years of age at the time, and must therefore have been born about the year 1649.

The only information now available concerning the future Viscount Dundee's early life, prior to his matriculation as a student, is supplied by the Roll of the Burgesses of Dundee, which sets forth that, on the 22nd of September 1660, 'John Graham of Claverhouse and David Graham, his brother, were admitted Burgesses and Brethren of the Guild of Dundee, by reason of their father's privilege.' The register of St Leonard's College establishes the fact that the two brothers went up together to the University of St Andrews towards the beginning of 1665.

This may be looked upon as a strong confirmation of the date which we have assigned as that of Claverhouse's birth. That he should begin his academic course in his twenty-second year and continue it up to the age of twenty-five, would have been quite contrary to the custom of a period when Scottish undergraduates, more particularly those belonging to the leading families of the country, were even more youthful than many of them are at the present day.

It has generally been assumed that Claverhouse remained at St Andrews for the full period of three years; but the University register supplies no evidence in support of this. On the contrary, the absence of John Graham's name from the list of those of his class-mates who graduated in due course, justifies the belief that his studies were brought to a premature close before 1668. To what extent he availed himself of the opportunities afforded him during such stay as he may have made at St Andrews, is a matter with regard to which proof is wholly wanting and testimony only bare and vague.

Dr Monro, the Principal of the College of Edinburgh, in his answer to the charge brought against him on the ground of 'his rejoicing the day that the news of Claverhouse his victory came to the town,' admitted that he had not 'rejoiced at the fall of my Lord Dundee,' for whom he 'had an extraordinary value'; and he challenged any 'gentleman, soldier, scholar or civilized citizen' to find fault with him for holding the fallen leader's memory in respect. From this, the utterance of one well qualified by personal acquaintance to form a competent judgment, and unlikely, from his training and education to express it in inconsiderate terms of meaningless exaggeration, it has been argued that the subject of Monro's eulogy must have possessed the attainments upon which men of culture naturally set store. In support of this warrantable inference, there is the statement of a writer who, though not a contemporary, is undeniably a well-informed chronicler. The author of the Memoirs of Sir Ewan Cameron says that Claverhouse 'had ane education suitable to his birth and genius.' According to the same authority, he 'made a considerable progress in the mathematicks, especially in those parts of it that related to his military capacity; and there was no part of the Belles Lettres which he had not studied with great care and exactness. He was much master in the epistolary way of writeing; for he not onely expressed himself with great ease and plaineness, but argued well, and had a great art in giving his thoughts in few words.'

Burnet, who, though a connection of Claverhouse's, is very far from displaying any partiality for him, allows that he was 'a man of good parts.' Dalrymple records that 'Dundee had inflamed his mind from his earliest youth, by the perusal of antient poets, historians and orators, with the love of the great actions they praise and describe.' Finally, there is the testimony of the 'officer' who wrote the 'Memoirs of Dundee' published in 1714, and who makes direct reference to his 'liberal education in humanity and in mathematicks.'

The question of Claverhouse's scholarship is not one of special moment in itself; yet it acquires some interest from the animated controversy to which it has given rise, and which originated in a hasty comment made by Sir Walter Scott. The novelist, after referring to a newly published letter, casually added, 'Claverhouse, it may be observed, spells like a chambermaid.' Subsequent writers, interpreting this into a general estimate of Dundee's educational acquirements, repeated the petty and irrelevant charge, in season and out of season, almost as though the quality of his orthography constituted a test by which his whole character was to be estimated. That Claverhouse was erratic in his spelling cannot be denied. It may be questioned, on the other hand, whether, in this respect, he displayed greater disregard for orthography than the average gentleman of his day. If he wrote 'I hop' for 'I hope,' 'deuk' for 'Duke,' 'seased' for 'seized,' 'fisik' for 'physic,' and 'childring' for 'children,' it does not require a very extensive acquaintance with the correspondence of the seventeenth century to know that dukes and earls, and even lawyers and divines, indulged in vagaries equally startling. But, if the arbitrary and occasionally whimsical spelling of his letters affords no proof of exceptional ignorance, the vigour, clearness, and directness of the style in which they are written give them a place rather above than below the epistolatory standard of the time.

After leaving St Andrews, Claverhouse, following the example set by so many generations of his countrymen, and notably by his illustrious kinsman, the Marquis of Montrose, repaired to the Continent, with the intention of devoting himself to a military career. According to his earliest biographer, 'an Officer of the Army,' he 'spent some time in the French service as a volunteer, with great reputation and applause.' This is repeated rather than confirmed by the author of the 'Memoirs of Sir Ewan Cameron of Lochiel,' with the addition, it is true, of the statement that it was 'under the famous Marishall Turenne' the young soldier received his first training. Dalrymple, without supplying precise information, records that Claverhouse 'entered the profession of arms with an opinion he ought to know the services of different nations, and the duties of different ranks,' that, 'with this view he went into several foreign services,' and that 'when he could not obtain a command,' he served as a volunteer.

The most trustworthy evidence in support of the statement that Claverhouse served and fought in the armies of France, is that of James Philip of Almerieclose, his standard-bearer at Killiecrankie, who, in later years, devoted a Latin epic to the memory and the praise of the gallant Graham. Referring to his hero, he says, 'The French camps on the Loire, where Orleans lifts her towers, and on the Seine, where her increased waters lave the city of Paris, have beheld him triumphant over the defeated enemy, stained with the blood-marks of relentless war.' The passage is, unfortunately, one in which the author has so obviously taken poetical liberty with historical facts, that his words cannot be taken literally. As the editor and translator of the poem points out, 'there could have been no fighting on the Seine or Loire.' Whether, on the other hand, it be probable that 'camps of instruction were there, from which young soldiers were sent to the front,' is a matter of little moment. Even without such explanation the passage is valuable as evidence. It may be accepted as definitively establishing the fact that it was in France Claverhouse first learnt the art of war.

It has been further conjectured that he may have belonged to the contingent of 6000 English and Scottish troops, which, under the leadership of Monmouth, joined Turenne's army in 1672. If such were the case, the duration of his service must have been brief. There is evidence to prove that, by the summer of 1674, he had transferred his allegiance to William of Orange, and that he was present at the battle of Seneff, fought in August of that year; and there are grounds for believing that he was directly instrumental in rescuing the Prince from a perilous situation.

Macaulay, it is true, rejects the story as 'invented' by some Jacobite many years after both William and Dundee were dead. That, however, appears to have been hastily done, on the erroneous assumption that the account of the alleged incident went no further back than the Memoirs of 1714. They, indeed, do state of Claverhouse, that, 'at the battle of St Neff, 1674, when the Prince of Orange was dismounted, and in great danger of being taken, he rescued him, and brought him off upon his own horse.' But this does not constitute the sole authority. In addition to it, there is that of the Memoirs of Lochiel. It is the more valuable that the author bases his own narrative on the Latin epic to which, in the following passage, he refers as one of the sources of his compilation. ' Besides the assistance I have from the Earl of Balcarres his memoirs of the wars, and the several relations I have had of them from many who were eyewitnesses, I have before me a manuscript copy of an historical Latin poem called "The Grameis," written in imitation of Lucan's "Pharsalia," but unfinished, by Mr Philips of Amryclos, who had the office of standard-bearer during that famous expedition' in the Highlands. From Philips he not only draws the incident of Seneff, but also gives a rough translation in English verse, of the passage commemorating this 'vigorous exploit.' It runs thus :—

> ' When the feirce Gaule, thro' Belgian stanks yow fled,
> Fainting, alone, and destitute of aid,
> While the proud victor urg'd your doubtfull fate,
> And your tir'd courser sunk beneath your weight,
> Did I not mount you on my vigorous steed,
> And save your person by his fatal speed ? '

Until recently, Philips' poem existed in manuscript only. That circumstance consequently gives the value of distinct contemporary evidence to another effusion, of which the author cannot be suspected of having drawn from the ' Grameis ' his allusion, unfortunately only a vague one, to the exploits of Claverhouse whilst serving under the Prince of Orange. Moreover, it was as early as January 1683, that is several years before the occurrence of the leading events celebrated in the ' Grameis,' that the anonymous rhymer published 'The Muse's New Year's Gift, and Hansell, to the right honoured Captain John Graham of Claverhouse.' In that poem the following lines are to be found :—

> 'I saw the man who at St Neff did see
> His conduct, prowess, martial gallantry :
> He wore a white plumach that day ; not one
> Of Belgians wore a white, but him alone ;
> And though that day was fatal, yet he fought,
> And for his part fair triumphs with him brought.'

Once, at least, during the period of his military service under the Dutch, Claverhouse returned to Scotland. He was in Edinburgh in March 1676. From there he wrote two letters to John Stewart, younger of Garntully, about the purchase of a horse and the gift of a 'setting dogue.' By the beginning of the following month he had again left the country ; for, in a letter written by his directions after his hurried departure, and dated the 4th of April, the hope is expressed that 'this day hie is in Holland.' He was not to continue in the pay of the States-General much longer. The very next year he resigned his commission, and came home to solicit employment in the British Army. To account for this apparently sudden determination, the author of the Memoirs of Lochiel relates a highly dramatic incident, for which, it must be added, there is no authority but his own, and of which the details are not such as to command unhesitating belief. After having given his account of William's rescue by Claverhouse, at Seneff, the chronicler continues :—

'The Prince, in reward of this service, gave him a Captain's commission, and promised him the first regiment that should fall in the way ; and some years thereafter, there happning a vacancy in one of the Scotch regiments, he stood candidate for it, not only upon the assurance of that promise, but also of the letters he procured from King Charles and the Duke of York, recommending him to the Prince, in very strong terms. But, notwithstanding of all this, the Prince preferred Mr Collier, a son of the Earl of

Portmore, to the regiment. The Prince then resided att his Palace of the Loo; and Captain Grahame, who was absent while this intrigue was carrying on, chanceing to meet Mr Collier in the Palace Court, expostulated the matter in very harsh terms, and gave him some blows with his cane.

'The Prince either saw or was soon informed of what passed, and ordering Captain Grahame, who had been seized by the officer of the guards, to be brought before him, he asked him how he dared to strick any person within the verge of his Palace? The Captain answered, that he was indeed in the wrong, since it was more his Highness his business to have resented that quarrel than his; because Mr Collier had less injured him in disappointing him of the regiment, than he had done his Highness in making him breck his word. Then replyed the Prince, in an angry tone, "I make yow full reparation, for I bestow on yow what is more valuable than a regiment, when I give yow your right arm!" The Captain subjoyned, that since his Highness had the goodness to give him his liberty, he resolved to employ himself elsewhere, for he would not serve a Prince longer that had brock his word.

'The Captain having thus thrown up his commission was preparing in haste for his voyage, when a messenger arrived from the Prince with two hundred guineas for the horse on which he had saved his life. The Captain sent the horse but ordered the gold to be distributed among the grooms of the Prince's stables. It is said, however, that his Highness had the generosity to wryte to the King and the Duke recommending him as a fine gentleman, and a brave officer, fitt for any office, civil or military.'

In the "Life of Lieutenant-General Hugh Mackay," the account given is more summary: 'About this time,' it is said, 'the lieutenant-colonelcy of one of the regiments, forming the Scottish brigade, falling vacant, two candidates started for the appointment. both excellent officers, but men of characters widely different. These were Graham of Claverhouse, then an officer in the Prince's service, afterwards notorious for his unrelenting cruelties to the Covenanters in the West of Scotland, and Mackay, characterised by Bishop Burnet, as the most pious military man he ever knew. The Prince preferred Mackay, which gave such mortal offence to his rival, that he instantly quitted the service and returned to Scotland, burning with resentment against the authors of his disappointment.'

Neither of these two narratives is contemporary. But the more circumstantial embodies the Jacobite legend current in the early years of the eighteenth century, whilst the briefer is founded on the tradition preserved in the family of Claverhouse's Whig opponent. The one point on which they both agree may therefore be accepted with some confidence; and it seems plausible to ascribe Captain Graham's withdrawal from the Dutch service to the dissatisfaction which he felt at the inadequate recognition of his claims to promotion.

Claverhouse experienced no difficulty in obtaining employment under his own sovereign. Two letters bearing on the subject have been preserved. They are both written by his relative, the Marquis of Montrose; one of them is addressed to him, the other to the Laird of Monorgan, who was also a Graham. The former is as follows :—

'FOR THE LAIRD OF CLAVERHOUSE.

'SIR,—You cannot imagine how overjoyed I should be, to have any employment at my disposal that were worthy of your acceptance; nor how much I am ashamed to offer you anything so far below your merit as that of being my Lieutenant; though I be fully persuaded that it will be a step to a much more considerable employment, and will give you occasion to confirm the Duke in the just and good opinion which I do assure you he has of you; he being a person that judges not of people's worth by the rank they are in.

'I do not know, after all this, in what terms, nor with what confidence, I can express my desire to have you accept this mean and inconsiderable offer; whether by endeavouring to magnify it all I can, and telling you, that it is the first troop of the Duke of York's regiment; that I am to raise it in Scotland; and that I pretend that none but gentlemen should ride in it; or, by telling you that I am promised to be very quickly advanced, and that you shall either succeed to me, or share with me in my advancement. I can say no more, but that you will oblige me in it beyond expression.

'I do not expect any answer to this while I am here; for I do resolve to be in Edinburgh against the first or second day of the next month; where, if you be not already, I earnestly entreat you would be pleased to meet me.—Sir, Your most affectionate cousin and servant,

'LONDON, *February* 19*th* [1677-8].'   MONTROSE.'

From this letter, it has been assumed that Claverhouse had previously made application to his kinsman and titular chief. There can, indeed, hardly be a doubt that it is a reply to a previous request. On the other hand, however, the second letter, written on the same day, does not altogether bear out this view. It was thus:—

'FOR THE LAIRD OF MONORGAN.

'SIR,—I hope now to be able, within a week or ten days, to give you an account, by word of mouth, of my resolutions, and the reasons I have for accepting a troop in the Duke of York's regiment of horse; so I shall forbear troubling you with a long letter; only I must tell you that I have all along met with a great deal of favour from his Royal Highness, and that he has assured me that this shall be but a step to a more considerable employment.

'He has a very good opinion of Claverhouse, and he bid me endeavour by all means to get him for my Lieutenant. Therefore, I most earnestly beg that you would be pleased to represent to him the advantages he may have by being near the Duke, and by making himself better known to him. And withal assure him from me, that, if he will embrace this offer, he shall also share with me in my advancement and better fortune. I need not use many words to show you the disparity that is betwixt serving under me and anybody else, though of greater family, he being of my house, and descended of my family.

'You may say more to this purpose than is fit for me to do. I shall say no more but that by this you will infinitely oblige.—Sir, Your most affectionate cousin and servant,   MONTROSE.'

'LONDON, *February* 19*th* [1677-8].'

It is not necessary to look upon this, with Napier, as 'conclusive against the conjecture that Claverhouse had *applied* for this service,' and as affording proof that the commission was spontaneously offered him in recognition of his military abilities. It is more plausible in itself, and more in accordance with the purport of both letters, to believe that Claverhouse had solicited employment from the Duke of York, with whom a recommendation from the Prince of Orange, who had lately become his son-in-law, was likely to possess considerable influence; that James had referred the applicant to the young Marquis, who was then raising a troop for the Duke's regiment of horse-guards; and that he had, at the same time urged Montrose to secure the services of an officer so brave and so able as Claverhouse had already shown himself to be.

It is not clear whether Claverhouse was really called upon to do duty as a mere subaltern. If so, it was but for a few months. As early as the 21st of November 1678, the Marquis of Montrose superseded the Marquis of Athole as commander of the Royal Horse Guards in Scotland; and the opportunity thus afforded of fulfilling the promise recently made to his kinsman was not neglected. Claverhouse was at once promoted to the vacant post, and thus began that part of his career which was to make him so prominent in the history of his country.

II

THE COVENANT AND THE COVENANTERS

ON the 14th of May 1678, a letter addressed to the King by his Privy Council in Scotland, contained a suggestion of which the adoption was destined to exercise an important influence on Claverhouse's career. It was written in answer to a prior communication, which it sufficiently explains, and ran as follows :—

'We have of late had divers informations of numerous field-conventicles kept in several places of the kingdom, who, with armed men, have in many places resisted your authority, and which by your letter, we find has reached your ears, and seeing these insolences are daily iterated, and are still upon the growing hand, and that your Majesty is graciously pleased to ask our advice, for raising of more forces,—It's our humble opinion that, for the present exigent, there may be two company of dragoons, each consisting of one hundred, presently raised, whose constant employment may be for dissipating and interrupting those rendezvouses of rebellion ; and therefore we have recommended to the Major-General, the speedy raising of them ; and your Majesty may be pleased to give commissions to such qualified persons as the Major-General hath, at our desire, given in a list, to command these two companies ; or to what other persons your Majesty shall think fit.'

In accordance with the advice conveyed in this letter, measures were forthwith taken for raising two additional companies. When formed and officered they were sent to join the troop which Claverhouse already commanded. At the head of this body of some three hundred men he was entrusted with the difficult task of 'dissipating and interrupting' the conventicles in the western and south-western districts of Scotland.

To understand the principles, motives, and aims of those against whom Claverhouse was now called upon to take action, it is necessary to recall the circumstances which accompanied and some of the events which followed the signing in 1643, of the 'Solemn League and Covenant for Reformation and Defence of Religion, the Honour and Happiness of the King, and the Peace and Safety of the three kingdoms of Scotland, England and Ireland.'

In the month of August of that year, the respective committees of the General Assembly and of the Convention of Estates had submitted to those bodies a draft of the document, as it had been drawn up by them, after consultation and deliberation with the Committee of the English Parliament. It had been duly sanctioned, and adopted as the most powerful means, by the blessing of God, for settling and preserving the true Protestant religion, with a perfect peace in all his Majesty's dominions, and propagating the same to other nations, and for establishing his Majesty's throne to all ages and generations.

Two months later—on the 11th of October—the commissioners of the General Assembly issued an ordinance for the solemn receiving, swearing, and subscribing of the League and Covenant. It contained special injunctions to the Presbyteries that they should take account of the performance thereof in their several bounds; that they should proceed with the censures of the Kirk against all such as should refuse or shift to swear and subscribe, as enemies to the preservation and propagation of religion; and that they should notify their names and make particular report of them to the Commission.

On the next day, the Commissioners of the Convention of Estates, in their turn issued a proclamation by which, supplementing the censures of the Church, they ordained as a penalty on those who should 'postpone or refuse,' that they should 'have their goods and rents confiscate for the use of the public,' and that they should not 'bruik nor enjoy any benefit, place nor office within this kingdom.'

The Covenant, which these ordinances thus required the people of Scotland to subscribe, consisted in an oath binding them to support the reformed religion in the Church of Scotland, in doctrine, worship, discipline and government, according to the Word of God, and the example of the best reformed Churches; to endeavour to bring the Churches of God in the three kingdoms to the nearest conjunction and uniformity in religion, confession of faith, form of Church government, directory for worship, and catechising; to strive, without respect of persons, for the extirpation of popery, prelacy (that is, Church government by archbishops, bishops, their chancellors and commissaries, deans and chapters, archdeacons, and all other ecclesiastical officers depending on that hierarchy), superstition, heresy, schism, profaneness and whatsoever should be found to be contrary to sound doctrine and the power of godliness; to endeavour to preserve the rights and privileges of the Parliaments, and the liberties of the kingdoms, and to preserve and defend the King's person and authority, in the preservation and defence of the true religion and liberties of the kingdoms; to endeavour to discover all such as had been, or should be, incendiaries, malignants, or evil instruments, by hindering the reformation of religion, dividing the King from his people, or one of the kingdoms from another, or making any factions or parties amongst the people, contrary to the League and Covenant, that they might be brought to public trial, and receive condign punishment, as the degree of their offences should require or deserve, or the supreme judicatories of both kingdoms, respectively, or others having power from them for that effect, should judge convenient; and, finally, to assist and defend all those that entered into this League and Covenant, and not to suffer themselves, directly or indirectly by whatsoever combination, persuasion, or terror, to be withdrawn from this blessed union and conjunction, whether to make defection to the contrary part, or to give themselves to a detestable indifference, or neutrality.

If, at its origin, the Covenant of 1643 was practically

a treaty between the heads of the Presbyterian party in Scotland and the leading Parliamentarians in England, it entered upon a new phase after the execution of Charles I. Notwithstanding the hostile attitude of the Presbyterians towards the King himself, they were strongly opposed to the subversion of the monarchical form of government. On the 5th of February, six days after the King's death, and one day earlier than the formal abolition of the monarchy by the English House of Commons, the Scottish Estates of Parliament passed an Act by which Prince Charles, then in Holland, was proclaimed King, in succession to his father. Following upon this, a deputation was sent to the Hague to invite Charles to come over and take possession of the throne of his ancestors. As a preliminary condition, however, it was required that he should give adhesion to the principles set forth in the Solemn Covenant. This he hesitated to do; and the commissioners returned, well pleased, indeed, with "the sweet and courteous disposition" of the Prince, but disappointed at the failure of their mission, owing to the pernicious influence of the "very evil generation, both of English and Scots," by whom he was surrounded.

A second deputation, sent shortly after this, to treat with the Prince at Breda, was more successful. Charles, seeing no other way open to him of regaining possession of the throne, gave his consent to the demands of the commissioners. In June 1650, he returned to Scotland. On the 1st of January 1651, he was crowned at Scone. Before taking the oath of coronation, and after the full text of the Solemn League and Covenant had been distinctly read to him, kneeling and lifting up his right hand, he assured and declared, on his oath, in the presence of Almighty God, the searcher of hearts, his allowance and approbation of all it set forth, and faithfully obliged himself to prosecute the ends it had in view, in his station and calling. He bound himself in advance to consent and agree to all Acts of Parliament establishing Presbyterial government; to observe their provisions in his own practice and family; and never to make opposition to them or endeavour to make any change in them.

It was not till nearly ten years later that Charles II. was really restored to the throne. The event was hailed with joy by the Presbyterians, who looked upon it as the accession of a covenanting king, and who founded their hopes, not only on the promise made at Scone, but also on a letter which Charles had forwarded, through Sharp, to the Presbytery of Edinburgh, to be communicated to all the Presbyteries in Scotland, and in which he expressed his resolve to protect and preserve the government of the Church of Scotland, as settled by law, without violation.

But the law itself was to be modified in such a manner as to enable the King to violate the spirit of his promise whilst leaving him a verbal quibble with which to justify his breach of faith. On the 9th of February an Act was passed annulling the Parliament and Committees of 1649, that is, declaring those proceedings to be illegal, by which Presbyterianism had been established on its firmest foundations. Less than three weeks later, two other Acts were passed with a view to preparing the way for a complete revolution in Church matters. The first of them, known as the Act Rescissory, had for its objects the annulling of the 'pretended Parliaments' of the years 1640, 1641, 1644, 1645 ,1646, and 1648—a measure which Principal Baillie described at the time as 'pulling down all our laws at once which concerned our Church since 1633.' The other, which purported to be 'concerning religion and Church government,' was substantially an assertion and recognition of the King's claim to be considered as head of the Church. It declared that it was his full and firm intention to maintain the true reformed Protestant religion in its purity of doctrine and worship, as it had been established within the kingdom during the reigns of his father and of his grandfather; to promote the power of godliness; to encourage the exercises of religion, both public and private; and to suppress all profaneness and disorderly walking; and that, for this end he would give all due countenance and protection to the ministers of the Gospel, 'they containing themselves within the bounds and limits of their ministerial calling and behaving themselves with that submission and obedience to his Majesty's authority and commands that is suitable to the allegiance and duty of good subjects.' A concluding clause provided that, notwithstanding the Rescissory Act, the 'present administration by sessions, presbyteries, and synods—they keeping within bounds and behaving themselves'—should, 'in the meantime' be 'allowed.'

The official toleration of Presbyterianism lasted till the 27th of May 1662. On that day an Act of Parliament, after declaring in its preamble that the ordering and disposal of the external government and policy of the Church properly belonged to the King, as an inherent right of the Crown, and by virtue of his royal prerogative and supremacy in causes ecclesiastical, proceeded to re-establish the ancient government of the Church by the sacred order of Bishops. A further step was taken on the 5th of September of the same year by the imposition of a test on all persons in public trust. Before entering upon the duties of any office under the Crown, they were called upon to subscribe a declaration setting forth that they judged it unlawful in subjects, under pretence of reformation, or for any motive, to enter into leagues and covenants; that they more especially considered the Solemn League and Covenant to have been contrary to the fundamental laws and liberties of the kingdom; and that they repudiated any obligation laid upon them by their former sworn recognition and acceptance of this bond.

As a sequel, an Act not of Parliament but of Council, ordained that the Covenant should be burnt by the hand of the common hangman. Prior to this, however, on the 11th of June 1662, an Act concerning such benefices and stipends as had been possessed without presentations from the lawful patrons deprived the Church of the right claimed by it of calling and choosing its own ministers. Under its provisions, no minister admitted subsequently to the year 1649 could possess any legal claim to his stipend unless he obtained a new presentation, and collation from the bishop of the diocese.

The number of those that consented to make the required application was so small that it was thought necessary to have recourse to the Privy Council for the purpose of enforcing the new law. On the 1st of October, an order was issued which deprived the recusant ministers of their parishes, and required them, with their families, to remove beyond the bounds of their respective presbyteries before the first day of the following November. The Archbishop of Glasgow, at whose instance this coercive measure was adopted, had asserted that there would not be ten in his diocese who refused compliance, under dread of such a penalty. The result falsified his prediction. Nearly four hundred ministers throughout Scotland abandoned their benefices, and subjected themselves and their families to the hardships and privations of banishment rather than recognise the new modelling of the Church.

In many cases the ejection of the ministers and the loss of their stipends did not prevent them from continuing the duties of their office. Secret meetings, either in private houses or in secluded localities, replaced the ordinary services of the Church. For the purpose of checking this violation of the law, the Council, on the 13th of August 1663, again intervened with an Act. It commanded and charged all ministers appointed in, or since, the year 1649, who had not subsequently obtained presentations from the patrons, and yet continued to preach or to exercise any duty proper to the functions of the ministry, either at the parish churches or in any other place, to remove themselves, their families and their goods, within twenty days, out of their respective parishes, and not to reside within twenty miles of them, nor within six miles of Edinburgh or any cathedral church, or three miles of any burgh within the kingdom.

In 1665, this Act was extended so as to include the older ministers, that is, those who had obtained their livings prior to the year 1649; and, on the same day, a proclamation against conventicles and meetings for religious exercises was published. It warned all such as should be present at these unlawful gatherings, that they would be looked upon as seditious persons, and should be punished by fining, confining and other corporal punishments, according to the judgment of the Privy Council, or any having the King's authority.

To replace the recusant clergy, a number of ministers, King's curates, as they were called, had been appointed by the bishops. They were so coldly received by the people that, to provide them with congregations, the Privy Council commanded all loyal subjects to frequent the ordinary meetings of public worship in their own parish churches ; and required magistrates to treat those who kept away as though they were Sabbath breakers, and to punish them by the infliction of a fine of twenty shillings for each absence. These measures having proved ineffective, the pecuniary penalty was greatly increased by a subsequent Act of Parliament. For refusing to recognise the curates, each nobleman, gentleman or heritor was to lose a fourth part of his yearly revenue ; every yeoman, tenant or farmer was to forfeit such a proportion of his free moveables (after the payment of the rents due to the master and landlord) as the Privy Council should think fit, but not exceeding a fourth part of them ; and every burgess was to be deprived of the privilege of merchandising and trading, and of all other 'liberties within burgh,' in addition to the confiscation of a fourth part of his moveable goods. Further, to prevent any evasion of the law against conventicles, proclamations issued at various times, prohibited all preaching and praying in families, if more than three persons, besides the members of the household, were present ; and made landlords, magistrates and heads of families answerable for the default of those under their charge to conform to the episcopal government and ritual.

It was not the intention of those who had instigated this coercive and penal legislation that it should remain a dead letter. As a means of enforcing obedience to it and of levying the fines imposed upon those who would not yield dutiful submission, troops were sent into the discontented districts. The south-western counties, in which the Covenanters were most numerous and most determined, were entrusted to Sir James Turner. His orders were to punish recalcitrant families by quartering his men on them, and, if they remained obstinate, to distrain their goods and gear, and to sell them in discharge of the fines incurred. It was the carrying out of these instructions that first led to armed resistance on the part of the Covenanters.

The immediate cause of the rising, however, is conflictingly stated by different writers. Kirkton's version of the occurrence, which has been reproduced almost literally by Wodrow, is to the effect that, on the 13th of November 1666, four of the men who had abandoned their homes on the appearance of the military, coming, in the course of their wanderings, towards the old clachan of Dalry, in Galloway, to seek refreshment after long fasting, providentially met, upon the highway, three or four soldiers driving before them a company of people, for the purpose of compelling them to thresh the corn of a poor old neighbour of theirs, who had also fled from his house, and from whom the church fines, as they were called, were to be exacted in this way. 'This,' says Kirkton, 'troubled the poor countrymen very much, yet they passed it in silence, till, coming to the house where they expected refreshment, they were informed the soldiers had seized the poor old man, and were about to bind him and set him bare upon a hot iron gird-iron, there to torment him in his own house. Upon this they ran to relieve the poor man, and coming to his house, desired the soldiers to let the poor man go, which the soldiers refused, and so they fell to words; whereupon two of the soldiers rushing out of the chamber with drawn swords, and making at the countrymen, had almost killed two of them behind their backs, and unawares; the countrymen having weapons, one of them discharged his pistol, and hurt one of the soldiers with the piece of a tobacco pipe with which he had loaded his pistol instead of ball. This made the soldiers deliver their arms and prisoner.'

The accuracy of the account given by Kirkton has been denied. Burnet distinctly asserts that 'this was a story made only to beget compassion'; that after the insurrection was quashed, the Privy Council sent commissioners to examine into the violences that had been committed, particularly in the parish where this was alleged to have been done; that he himself read the report they made to the Council, and all the depositions taken by them from the people of the district, but that no such violence on the part of the military was mentioned in any one of them. The wounded soldier himself, one George Deanes, a corporal in Sir Alexander Thomson's company, from whose body ten pieces of tobacco pipe were subsequently extracted by the surgeon, told Sir James Turner that he was shot because he would not take the covenanting oath.

Whether premeditated and concerted, or merely 'an occasional tumult upon a sudden fray,' this attack on the military was the signal for a gathering of the discontented peasantry of the district. On the morrow, the four countrymen, one of whom was M'Lelland of Boscob, being joined by six or seven others, fell upon a second party of soldiers. One of these, having offered resistance was killed; his comrades, about a dozen in number, according to Kirkton, quietly gave up their arms. Within two days the insurgents had recruited about fourscore horse and two hundred foot. Proceeding to Dumfries, where Turner then lay with only a few of his soldiers, the greater number of them being scattered about the country in small parties, for the purpose of levying the fines, they seized him, together with the papers and the money in his possession, and carried him off as a prisoner. After this, 'in their abundant loyalty,' as Wodrow characterises it, they went to the Cross and publicly drank to the health of the King and the prosperity of his Government.

In daily increasing numbers the insurgents marched towards Edinburgh. At Lanark, where all the contingents they could expect from the south and west had already joined them, and where 'this rolling snow-ball was at the biggest,' they were estimated at some three thousand. Here they renewed the Solemn League and Covenant. In spite of repeated warnings from men who, whilst fully sympathising with them, yet understood the hopeless nature of the enterprise in which they were engaged, the leaders determined to push on towards the capital. But the enthusiasm of many amongst their followers was beginning to wane; and by the time Colinton was reached, the ill-armed and undisciplined crowd had dwindled down again to a bare thousand. Then at length, even those who had previously rejected the well-meant advice of their more cautious friends, and had declared that, having been called by the Lord to this undertaking, they would not retire till he who bade them come should likewise command them to go, became conscious of their desperate plight, and consented to a retreat towards the west. Turning the eastern extremity of the Pentland hills, they directed their march towards Biggar.

But it was too late. Dalziel, the governor of Edinburgh, who, at the head of a hastily mustered body of regulars, had been sent out to intercept them, came upon them at Rullion Green, on the evening of the 28th of November. A sharp engagement followed. Twice in the course of it success seemed to favour the insurgents; but in the end the military training and the superior weapons of their opponents prevailed, and the Covenanters were scattered in headlong flight. Of the soldiers, only five fell. On the other side there were about forty killed and a hundred and thirty taken. These prisoners were next day marched into Edinburgh. They might all have saved their lives if they had consented to renounce the Covenant; but their refusal to do so was severely punished. According to Burnet, who certainly does not exaggerate the number who suffered the death penalty, ten were hanged upon one gibbet in Edinburgh, and thirty-five more were sent to be hanged up before their own doors. Many were transported across the seas. The torture of the boot and of the thumbkins—the latter said to have been introduced by Dalziel, who had learnt their use in Russia, where he served for a time—was freely applied in the hope of wringing from the prisoners the admission that the rising was part of a concerted plot for the subversion of the existing government. They all strenuously denied it.

That shortly prior to this, a conspiracy had been formed

for this object is a well established fact.   A document
discovered by Dr M'Crie in the Dutch archives and published by him in his edition of the Memoirs of Veitch,
shows that a plan was formed, in July 1666, for seizing on
the principal forts in the kingdom, and that 'the persons
embarked in this scheme had carried on a correspondence
with the Government of the United Provinces then at war
with Great Britain, and received promises of assistance
from that quarter.'   Another document referred to by the
same writer asserts that the castles of Edinburgh, Stirling,
and Dumbarton were amongst those to be taken possession
of.   Whether this Dutch plot and the Galloway insurrection were connected with each other, is a point with regard
to which historians have maintained conflicting opinions
in accordance with their own sympathies.   The strongest
evidence that Napier is able to adduce, on the one side,
is the fact that a Mr Wallace is mentioned as one of those
in correspondence with Holland, and that Colonel James
Wallace was the leader of the insurgents whom Dalziel
routed at Rullion Green.   But, on the other hand, it is
pointed out by Dr M'Crie that, as the other names are
obviously fictitious, this coincidence affords no ground
for supposing that the Colonel was the person referred to.

For many months after the Pentland rout, the harrying
of the late insurgents continued; but, at length, the
political changes which placed the administration of the
country into the hands of Lauderdale, also marked the
inauguration of a more lenient policy towards the Presbyterians.   On the 15th of July 1669, a letter was communicated to the Council, in which the King signified his
desire that it should authorise as many of the ejected
ministers as had lived peaceably in the places where they
had resided, to return and preach, and exercise the other
functions of their office in the parish churches which they
formerly occupied, providing these were vacant.   Ministers
who took collation from the bishop of the diocese and kept
presbyteries and synods, might be allowed to receive their
stipends.   The others were not to be permitted ' to meddle

with the local stipend, but only to possess the manse and glebe.'

This concession proved of little effect. The few who availed themselves of the 'Indulgence'—two and forty in all, according to Wodrow—were looked upon as renegades by the irreconcilables, and found no more toleration at their hands than the curates had done. The moderate Presbyterians who accepted the 'indulged' clergy were denounced as traitors to the cause. The conventicles which it had been hoped the new measure would suppress, began to assume a more desperate character, as the gatherings of those who, in their unbending determination to abide by the very letter of the Covenant, declared themselves freed from their allegiance to a king whom they considered as perjured, and against whose agents, as malignant persecutors of the true religion, they believed themselves justified in adopting the most violent measures. It is of these extremists that the covenanting party now consisted.

It has been urged that these new developments were too natural, in the circumstances of the time, not to have been anticipated, by some, at least, of those who were responsible for the government of the country. They have consequently been credited with the deliberate intention not only of causing a disruption in the ranks of the Presbyterians, but also of making the expected refusal of the indulgence a pretext for further and sterner measures of coercion. If such were the case, the machiavellian policy was successful. Within six months, the old system of penal legislation was again adopted. On the 3rd of February 1670, a proclamation prohibiting conventicles under heavy penalties was issued by the Council. It was followed in August by an Act of Parliament which made it illegal for outed ministers not licensed by the Council or for any other persons not authorised or tolerated by the bishop of the diocese, to preach, expound Scripture, or pray in any meeting, except in their own houses and to members of their own family. Such as should be convicted of disobedience to this law were to be imprisoned till they found security, to the amount of five thousand

C

merks, for their future good behaviour.   Persons attending meetings of this kind were to be heavily fined, according to their respective conditions, for each separate offence. Against outdoor meetings, or 'field conventicles,' the law was still more severe.   Death was to be the penalty for preaching or praying at them, or even for convening them. A reward of five hundred merks was offered to any of his Majesty's subjects who should seize and secure the person of an active conventicler.   As a further inducement, a subsequent proclamation made over to the captor the fine incurred by the offender he secured.

Amongst the many devices resorted to at this time, with a view to enforcing conformity, there is one which, because of its immediate consequences, is deserving of special mention.   In October 1677, the Council addressed a letter to the Earls of Glencairn and Dundonald and to Lord Ross, requiring them to call together the heritors of the shires of Ayr and Renfrew, and to urge on them the necessity for taking effective measures to repress conventicles.   The answer given to the three noblemen and forwarded by them to Edinburgh was practically a refusal though it took the form of a plea of inability on the part of those whose co-operation had thus been invoked.   This alleged powerlessness was made an excuse for the next step taken by the Government, that of quartering a body of eight thousand Highlanders in the disaffected counties, on those who refused to subscribe a bond by which every heritor made himself answerable, not only for his wife, children, and servants, but also for his tenants.

The commission for raising the Highlanders authorised them to take free quarters, and, if need were, to seize on horses as well as on ammunition and provisions.   They were indemnified against all pursuits, civil and criminal, which might at any time be intented against them or anything they should do, by killing, wounding, apprehending, or imprisoning such as should make opposition to the King's authority, or by arresting such as they might have reason to suspect.   For two months the clansmen availed themselves to the full of the arbitrary powers with which the

royal warrant invested them. At length the Duke of
Hamilton appealed directly to the King to put an end to
the oppression exercised in his name by the Highland men ;
and an express was sent down from London, requiring the
Council to disband them and to send them back to their
homes. This brings events down to 1678, the year in which
Claverhouse was appointed to the command of the dragoons
who were to make another effort to disperse the conventicles
against which so many Acts of Parliament and decrees of
Council had been directed in vain, and which even the
depredations of the Highland host had failed to check.

III

DISPERSING THE CONVENTICLERS

By the end of 1678 Claverhouse was at Moffat, expecting to be joined by one of the newly-levied troops of dragoons —that under Captain Inglis. From that town he forwarded to the Earl of Linlithgow, Commander-in-chief of the King's forces, the first of a series of despatches which contain a precise and detailed account of his movements at this time. As indicating the spirit in which he had undertaken the duties assigned to him, and the strict and literal obedience to orders that characterised his execution of them, the document is both interesting and valuable. It is dated the 28th of December, and runs as follows :—

'MY LORD,—I came here last night with the troop, and am just going to march for Dumfries, where I resolve to quarter the whole troop. I have not heard anything of the dragoons, though it be now about nine o'clock, and they should have been here last night, according to your Lordship's orders. I suppose they must have taken some other route. I am informed, since I came, that this country has been very loose. On Tuesday was eight days, and Sunday, there were great field-conventicles just by here, with great contempt of the regular clergy, who complain extremely when I tell them I have no orders to apprehend anybody for past misdemeanours. And besides that, all the particular orders I have being contained in that order of quartering, every place where we quarter must see them, which makes them fear the less. I am informed that the most convenient post for quartering the dragoons will be Moffat, Lochmaben and Annan ; whereby the whole country may be kept in awe. Besides that, my Lord, they

tell me that the end of the bridge of Dumfries is in Galloway; and that they may hold conventicles at our nose and
we not dare to dissipate them, seeing our orders confine
us to Dumfries and Annandale. Such an insult as that would
not please me; and, on the other hand, I am unwilling to
exceed orders, so that I expect from your Lordship orders
how to carry in such cases. I send this with one of my
troop, who is to attend orders till he be relieved. I will
send one every Monday, and the dragoons one every
Thursday, so that I will have the happiness to give your
Lordship account of our affairs twice a week, and your
Lordship occasion to send your commands for us as often.
In the meantime, my Lord, I shall be doing, according to
the instructions I have, what shall be found most advantageous for the King's service, and most agreeable to your
Lordship.—I am, my Lord, your Lordship's most humble
and obedient servant, J. GRAHAME.'

'My Lord, if your Lordship give me any new orders, I
will beg they may be kept as secret as possible; and sent
to me so suddenly as the information some of the favourers
of the fanatics are to send may be prevented, which will
extremely facilitate the executing of them.'

On the 6th of January 1679, Claverhouse, now at
Dumfries, again addressed a despatch to the Commander.
He appears to have, in the meantime, received an explanation of the Council's intention, and an intimation that
his conscientious regard for the exact terms of his commission did not meet with unqualified approval. This
may be gathered from the following paragraph in his
letter :—

'My Lord, since I have seen the Act of Council, the
scruple I had about undertaking anything without the
bounds of these two shires, is indeed frivolous, but was not
so before. For if there had been no such Act, it had not
been safe for me to have done anything but what my order
warranted; and since I knew it not, it was to me the same
thing as if it had not been. And for my ignorance of it,
I must acknowledge that till now, in any service I have

been in, I never enquired farther in the laws, than the orders of my superior officers.'

In another passage, having to report various incidents of recent occurrence, with respect to some of which it was intended to make formal complaint, he again gives proof of his respect for discipline, and manifests his determination not only to enforce it, but also to compensate those upon whom injury might be inflicted by any breach of it on the part of the men under his command. At the same time, he does not hesitate to make it clearly understood that, whilst ready to answer for his own conduct, he repudiates responsibility for the actions of others. His own words are as follows :—

'On Saturday night, when I came back here, the sergeant who commands the dragoons in the Castle came to see me ; and while he was here, they came and told me there was a horse killed just by, upon the street, by a shot from the Castle. I went immediately and examined the guard, who denied point blank that there had been any shot from thence. I went and heard the Bailie take depositions of men that were looking on, who declared, upon oath, that they saw the shot from the guard-hall, and the horse immediately fall. I caused also search for the bullet in the horse's head, which was found to be of their calibre. After that I found it so clear, I caused seize upon him who was ordered by the sergeant in his absence to command the guard, and keep him prisoner till he find out the man,—which I suppose will be found himself. His name is James Ramsay, an Angusman, who has formerly been a lieutenant of horse, as I am informed. It is an ugly business, for, besides the wrong the poor man has got in losing his horse, it is extremely against military discipline to fire out of a guard. I have appointed the poor man to be here to-morrow, and bring with him some neighbours to declare the worth of the horse, and have assured him to satisfy him if the Captain, who is to be here to-morrow, refuse to do it. I am sorry to hear of another accident that has befallen the dragoons, which I believe your Lordship knows better than I, seeing they say that there is a complaint made of it to your Lordship or the Council ;

which is, that they have shot a man in the arm with small shot, and disenabled him of it, who had come this length with a horse to carry baggage for some of my officers; but this being before they came to Moffat, does not concern me.

'The Stewart-Depute, before good company, told me that several people about Moffat were resolved to make a complaint to the Council against the dragoons for taking free quarters; that if they would but pay their horse-corn and their ale, they should have all the rest free; that there were some of the officers that had, at their own hand, appointed themselves locality above three miles from their quarter. I begged them to forbear till the Captain and I should come there, when they should be redressed in everything. Your Lordship will be pleased not to take any notice of this, till I have informed myself upon the place.

'This town is full of people that have resetted, and lodged constantly in their houses intercommuned persons and field preachers. There are some that absent themselves for fear; and Captain Inglis tells me there are Bailies have absented themselves there at Annan, and desired from me order to apprehend them; which I refused, for they are not included in all the Act of Council. Mr Cupar, who is here Bailie and Stewart for my Lord Stormont, offered to apprehend Bell that built the meeting-house, if I would concur. I said to him that it would be acceptable, but that the order from the Council did only bear the taking up the names of persons accessory to the building of it.'

The meeting-house referred to was situated in the neighbourhood of Castlemilk, and had been built at the expense of the common purse of the disaffected. It is described as a good large house, about sixty feet in length and between twenty and thirty in breadth, with only one door and with two windows at each side, and one at either end. After its purpose had become known to the authorities, it was fitted up with stakes and with a 'hek' and manger, to make it pass for a byre. In spite of this, an order for its destruction was issued by the Privy Council, shortly before Claverhouse's arrival in the district.

The first duty he was called upon to perform was that of supplying the squad that was to serve as an escort to James Carruthers, the Stewart-Depute, who had been commissioned to carry out the order. The dragoons themselves took no part in the actual demolition; but their presence was necessary, not only to overawe resistance, but also to compel the 'four score of countrymen, all fanatics,' whom Carruthers brought with him, to pull down the building. 'The Stewart-Depute,' Claverhouse reported, 'performed his part punctually enough. The walls were thrown down, and timber burnt. So perished the charity of many ladies.'

In subsequent despatches Claverhouse gives the most minute particulars as to the manner in which he has carried out his orders for the apprehension of various persons; and does not spare his comments on the lack of adequate support in the discharge of his arduous and ungrateful duties. A point upon which he lays great stress is the insufficiency of the arrangements made for supplying his men with proper quarters and with forage for their horses. He was obliged, he said, to let the dragoons quarter at large; and he was convinced that this was extremely improper at a time when the Council seemed resolved to proceed vigorously against the disaffected. He thought it strange, too, that they who had the honour to serve the King should have to pay more for hay and straw than would be asked from any stranger. He was determined for his part, that his troop should not suffer from the neglect or indifference of the commissioners appointed to treat with him. Though very unwilling to disoblige any gentleman, if his men ran short, he would go to any of the commissioners' lands that were near, and requisition what was required, offering the current rates in payment. This, he thought, was a step which he was justified in taking, and he was ready to defend his conduct if called upon to do so.

Another serious ground for complaint was the want of

proper information. Good intelligence, he said, was the thing most wanted. The outlawed ministers, men like Welsh of Irongray, were preaching within twenty or thirty miles, yet nothing could be done for want of spies to bring timely and trustworthy information concerning their movements. On the other hand, the conventiclers received regular and speedy knowledge of any expedition intended against them. There was reason to suppose that their informants were sometimes the troopers entrusted with orders. Of the treachery of one of these, who did not deliver till the twentieth a despatch dated the fifteenth, he was so convinced that, had it not been for the man's influential patrons, he would have turned him out of the troop with infamy, instead of merely putting him under arrest. The result of such insufficient and unsatisfactory service was well exemplified in the case of a number of persons whom he had been instructed to seize in Galloway. He had set out the very night he received his orders, and had covered forty miles of country. Of those for whom search was made, only two were apprehended, and that because they refused to take the same precautions as the rest for their safety. 'The other two Bailies were fled, and their wives lying above the clothes in the bed, and great candles lighted, waiting for the coming of the party, and told them they knew of their coming, and had as good intelligence as they themselves; and that if the other two were seized on, it was their own faults, that would not contribute for intelligence.'

Claverhouse's complaints produced but slight effect, though they were repeated until he grew weary of making them. Failing to obtain satisfaction, he bluntly declared that he would never solicit more, but that, if the King's service suffered in consequence, he would let the blame lie where it should.

About this time, however, an important measure, and one which brought down upon him the jealous displeasure of the Marquis of Queensberry, who resented it as an infringement of his rights, was adopted in Claverhouse's favour. Even if all the magistrates in the disaffected districts had been men of unimpeachable loyalty to the Government, the necessity for obtaining their co-operation would frequently have hampered and delayed the military authorities. But many of them were soon discovered to be lukewarm partisans at best; whilst not a few, if they did not openly side with the conventiclers, aided and abetted them by a deliberate and studied inactivity. To remedy this, and to give Claverhouse freer hand, he was, in March 1679, appointed sheriff-depute of the shires of Dumfries and Wigtown, and also of the stewartries of Annandale and Kirkcudbright. Andrew Bruce of Earls-hall, the lieutenant of his own troop of horse, was given him as a colleague. They were not, however, wholly to supersede the sheriffs previously in office, but only to sit with those judges or to supply them in their absence. Moreover, their powers were limited to putting the laws into execution only against withdrawers from the public ordinances, keepers of conventicles, and such as were guilty of disorderly baptisms and marriages, resetting and communing with fugitives, and intercommuned persons and vagrant preachers.

Claverhouse had not been long in the exercise of his twofold duties before he began to realise that his efforts were far from producing the desired results. Not only were conventicles as numerous as before, but there were also signs which convinced him that passive resistance was not all he would soon have to encounter. In a despatch which he wrote from Dumfries on the 21st of April 1679, he informed the Earl of Linlithgow that Mr Welsh was accustoming both ends of the country to face the King's force, and certainly intended to break out into an open rebellion. In view of this, he pointed out that the arms of the militia in Dumfriesshire as well as in Wigtownshire and Annandale, were in the hands of the country people, though very disaffected; and that those taken from the stewartry were in the custody of the town of Kirkcudbright, the most irregular place in the kingdom. He consequently suggested that they should be entrusted to his keeping, and also that his own men should be provided with more suitable weapons, those which they had got from the Castle being worth nothing.

A few days later, Lord Ross, writing from Lanark, conveyed a similar warning. He could learn nothing, he said, but of an inclination to rise, although there were none yet actually in arms. This was on the 2nd of May. On the 5th he forwarded another despatch in which he had to report an encounter between a small party of troopers and some peasants of the district. The soldiers had been sent out to apprehend a man who was reported to have in his possession some of the 'new-fashioned arms,' that is, halberts which were provided with a cleek, or crooked knife, for the purpose of cutting the dragoons' bridles, and of which the manufacture was in itself an indication of what was intended. After seizing the young fellow, who did not deny that he had been enlisted as one of those who were to defend the conventicles in arms, the troopers, instead of returning with their prisoner stabled their horses and fell a-drinking. Some of the neighbours, availing themselves of the opportunity, attacked them with forks, and the like, and wounded one of them 'very desperately ill.'

The next day Claverhouse also forwarded his report from Dumfries. It contained, in addition to an account of his own movements, the following comment on orders which he had just received, and which indicated that the Earl of Linlithgow was also alive to the dangers of the situation :—

'My Lord, I have received an order yesterday from your Lordship, which I do not know how to go about on a sudden, as your Lordship seems to expect. For I know not what hand to turn to, to find those parties that are in arms. I shall send out to all quarters, and establish spies ; and shall endeavour to engage them Sunday next, if it be possible. And if I get them not here' I shall go and visit them in Teviotdale or Carrick ; where they say, they dare look honest men in the face.'

On the 3rd of May, a few days before Lord Ross and Claverhouse drew up their respective reports, there had

happened an event which was destined to bring matters
to an immediate crisis, and which proved the signal for
another, and a far more serious rising than that of 1666.
James Sharp, Archbishop of St Andrews and Primate of
Scotland, was murdered on Magus Muir, by a party of
Covenanters.

Of this terrible tragedy, each side has its own account.
On the one hand, there is that which is based on the
narrative subsequently drawn up by Russell, one of the
leading actors in it. According to this version, no premeditation existed on the part of the nine men concerned.
They were in search of William Carmichael, the Sheriff-
depute of Fifeshire, a man who had made himself obnoxious
by the unrelenting severity which he displayed in carrying
out the laws against the Covenanters. Having missed
him, they were about to separate, when information was
brought them that Sharp's carriage was approaching.
Interpreting this into 'a clear call from God to fall upon
him,' they there and then resolved ' to execute the justice
of God upon him for the innocent blood he had shed.'

But if the Archbishop's murder was not determined upon
until the actual moment when circumstances cast him into
the hands of his enemies, Russell's account shows that it
had been discussed a short time prior to its perpetration.
He states that, on the 11th of April, a meeting was held
to consider what course should be taken with Carmichael
to scare him from his cruel courses ; that it was decided
to fall upon him at St Andrews ; and that when 'some
objected, what if he should be in the prelate's house, what
should be done in such a case, all present judged duty to
hang both over the post, especially the Bishop, it being by
many of the Lord's people and ministers judged a duty
long since, not to suffer such a person to live, who had
shed and was shedding so much of the blood of the saints,
and knowing that other worthy Christians had used means
to get him upon the road before.' He further represents
himself as urging the murder of Sharp, in the course of the
hurried consultation held as the primate's carriage was
approaching, on the ground that ' he had before been at

several meetings with several godly men in other places of the kingdom, who not only judged it their duty to take that wretch's life, and some others, but had essayed it twice before.'

Whilst it would appear from this account that no definite plan had been formed, to be carried out on the 3rd of May, though some of the more desperate of the Covenanters had come to a general understanding not to neglect any favourable opportunity 'to execute the justice of God' upon the wretch whom the Lord delivered into their hands, the other version, accepting the official narrative published immediately after the murder, asserts a distinct and premeditated purpose on the part of the assassins. It founds this on the 'informations' which were sent from St Andrews to the Privy Council, and which purported to embody the evidence of persons alleged to have been in communication with the men who perpetrated the crime.

In these it was stated that his Grace was waylaid by divers parties and could not escape, whether he went straight to St Andrews or repaired to his house at Scotscraig; that three days before the murder, several of those concerned in it met in Magask, at the house of John Miller, one of the witnesses, where they concerted the business; that the next night they put up with Robert Black, another witness, whose wife was a great instigator of the deed; that at parting, when one of them kissed her, the woman prayed that God might bless and prosper them, adding, 'if long Leslie'—the episcopalian minister of Ceres —'be with him, lay him on the green also,' to which the favoured individual whom she more particularly addressed, holding up his hand, answered, 'this is the hand that shall do it'; and that further, on the morning of the 3rd of May, the nine men followed the coach for a considerable distance, intending to attack it, first on the heath to the south of Ceres, and then at the double dykes of Magask, though owing to various circumstances, duly detailed, they did not get what seemed an available opportunity of doing so until it reached Magus Muir.

Standing thus, the question of premeditation gave rise to

a long and acrimonious controversy in which recrimina-
tions and invectives were freely bandied, and which, being
characterised, on either side, rather by a determination to
uphold a preconceived opinion than by a desire to arrive
at the plain truth, naturally led to no satisfactory conclusion.

The murder of Archbishop Sharp was followed by further
proclamations against the Covenanters, to whom, as a body,
the Government attributed the crime; and the episcopalian
agents throughout the country, actuated partly by a desire
for revenge, partly by fear for their own safety, displayed
increased zeal in carrying out the repressive enactments of
the Privy Council. This was met on the other side with
corresponding measures for self-defence. Even before the
tragedy at Magus Muir, a determination to repel force by
force had been noted and reported, and conventicles had
ceased to be merely peaceful gatherings of unarmed men.
They now began to assume the appearance of military camps,
to which the numerous smaller congregations that joined
together for mutual protection gave formidable proportions.

That with a view to bringing matters to an issue and
saving themselves by a general rising, Balfour and the
other outlaws who had fled as he had, for protection,
to the west, after the murder of the primate, were further
instrumental in stirring up a spirit of rebellion, scarcely
admits of doubt, and is, indeed, conceded by Wodrow.
But it is probable that they only helped to precipitate
what would not long have been delayed under any circumstances, and what Robert Hamilton, brother to the Laird
of Preston, and others who, like him, were violently opposed
to the indulgence, had for some time been working to
bring about. Towards the end of May, these men put
forth a manifesto, in which they declared it to be their
duty 'to publish to the world their testimony to the truth
and cause which they owned, and against the sins and
defections of the times.'

In accordance with this proclamation, they decided that
a party of armed men should go to some public place and
burn the Acts of Parliament passed since 1660 'for over-
turning the whole covenanted reformation.' Amongst these ·

was included 'that presumptuous Act for imposing an holy anniversary day to be kept yearly upon the 29th of May, as a day of rejoicing and thanksgiving for the King's birth and restoration,' whereby the appointers had 'intruded upon the Lord's prerogative,' and the observers had 'given the glory to the creature that is due to our Lord Redeemer, and rejoiced over the setting up an usurping power to the destroying the interest of Christ in the land.'

The 29th of May was at hand; and it was thought fitting that the obnoxious anniversary should witness the public protest and demonstration. Glasgow was the place originally chosen for the 'declaration and testimony of some of the true Presbyterian party in Scotland,' and for burning 'the sinful and unlawful Acts' passed against them, just as their own 'sacred covenant' had been burned. But a considerable number of the royal troops previously quartered in Lanark having been sent up to the city, it was thought prudent to go no nearer to it than Rutherglen. A party of the irreconcilables accordingly marched to the royal burgh. After burning the hated Acts in the bonfire with which the day was being solemnised, they put it out as a further protest against the celebration, publicly read their own declaration and testimony, and affixed a copy of it to the Market Cross.

On that same Thursday, Claverhouse, now at Falkirk, sent the Earl of Linlithgow a despatch containing the following paragraph :—

'I am certainly informed there is a resolution taken among the Whigs, that eighteen parishes shall meet Sunday next in Kilbride Moor, within four miles of Glasgow. I resolve, though I do not believe it, to advertise my Lord Ross, so that with our joint force we may attack them. They say they are to part no more, but keep in a body.'

At once taking measure to carry out the plan thus indicated, Claverhouse set out for Glasgow. On his way he received information of the proceedings at Rutherglen Cross, and thought it his duty to proceed, with his men, to the scene of the demonstration. The sequel is told in the next despatch to the Earl of Linlithgow :—

'GLASGOW, *June* 1st, 1679.

'MY LORD,—Upon Saturday's night, when my Lord
Rosse came into this place, I marched out; and because of
the insolency that had been done two nights before at
Ruglen, I went thither, and inquired for the names. So soon
as I got them, I sent out parties to seize on them, and
found not only three of those rogues, but also an intercommuned minister called King. We had them at Strathaven
about six in the morning yesterday; and resolving to convey
them to this, I thought that we might make a little tour, to
see if we could fall upon a conventicle; which we did little
to our advantage. For, when we came in sight of them,
we found them drawn up in battle, upon a most advantageous ground, to which there was no coming but
through mosses and lakes.

'They were not preaching, and had got away all their
women and children. They consisted of four battalions of
foot and all well armed with fusils and pitchforks, and three
squadrons of horse. We sent both parties to skirmish; they
of foot and we of dragoons: They run for it, and sent down
a battalion of foot against them: We sent threescore of
dragoons, who made them run shamefully: But, in the end
(they perceiving that we had the better of them in skirmish),
they resolved a general engagement, and immediately
advanced with their foot, the horse following: They came
through the loch, and the greatest body of all made up against
my troop: We kept our fire till they were within ten pace of
us: They received our fire, and advanced to shock: The
first they gave us brought down the Cornet Mr Crafford
and Captain Bleith: Besides that, with a pitchfork, they
made such an opening in my sorrel horse's belly, that his
guts hung out half an ell; and yet he carried me off a mile;
which so discouraged our men, that they sustained not the
shock, but fell into disorder.

'Their horse took the occasion of this, and pursued us so
hotly that we got no time to rally. I saved the standards;
but lost on the place about eight or ten men, besides
wounded. But the dragoons lost many more. They are
not come easily off on the other side, for I saw several of

them fall before we came to the shock. I made the best retreat the confusion of our people would suffer ; and am now laying with my Lord Ross. The town of Strathaven drew up as we was making our retreat, and thought of a pass to cut us off; but we took courage and fell on them, made them run, leaving a dozen on the place. What these rogues will do, yet I know not ; but the country was flocking to them from all hands. This may be counted the beginning of the rebellion, in my opinion.—I am, my Lord, your Lordship's most humble servant,   J. GRAHAME.'

'My Lord, I am so wearied, and so sleepy, that I have written this very confusedly.'

As to the respective numbers of the combatants engaged in the battle of Drumclog, as it is commonly called from the place near which it was fought, and which Claverhouse forgot to name in his despatch, it is difficult to arrive at a definite conclusion. Russell, who was in the ranks of the Covenanters, sets down the 'honest party' as consisting of 'about fifty horse and about as many guns, and about a hundred and fifty with forks and halberts'; but that is not consistent with the details which he himself gives of the fighting. Sir Walter Scott, who has been followed by most modern writers, computes the forces opposed to Claverhouse at about one thousand, horse and foot, and the regulars at no more than two hundred and fifty. But even this estimate of the latter is probably excessive. In a letter written from Mugdock on the 30th of May, the Marquis of Montrose informed the Earl of Menteith that he had that day met with Claverhouse, who had been sent 'with his troop and a troop of dragoons, to guard some arms and ammunition transported to this country.' That may be taken to mean an escort of about two hundred men. But Captain Creichton, who was then serving as a lieutenant under Claverhouse, states that he, with Captain Stewart's troop of dragoons remained in Glasgow, when his commanding officer set out to enquire into the Rutherglen demonstration ; and he adds that those who fought at Drumclog were about one hundred and eighty strong

Apart from the fact that there is no reason for doubting his veracity, the number which he gives exactly agrees with that which may be deduced from the casual reference in Montrose's letter; and there is, consequently, good reason for accepting it as correct. With regard to the insurgents, it is less easy to make even an approximative calculation. It is generally admitted, however, that they greatly outnumbered their adversaries; and this seems implied by the despatch which Lord Ross forwarded to the commander-in-chief immediately after Claverhouse's return to Glasgow on the memorable Sunday. 'Be assured,' he wrote to the Earl, 'if they were ten to one, if you command it, we shall be through them if we can.' Moreover, it is difficult to believe that the Covenanting forces could have increased to some six thousand within a week after Drumclog, as Hamilton, one of their leaders, boasts they did, if, on the 1st of June, they numbered no more than the mere handful of Russell's estimate.

The passage in which Claverhouse mentions the officers killed in the engagement has always been read as referring to only two; and it has caused some surprise that he should have omitted to report the loss of a third, about whose death there cannot be a doubt, and who, moreover, was a kinsman of his—Cornet Graham. Captain Creichton who, it must be remembered, is speaking of a comrade, and whose words alone might be looked upon as absolutely authoritative, states, in his Memoirs, that 'the rebels finding the cornet's body, and supposing it to be that of Clavers, because the name of Graham was wrought in the shirt-neck, treated it with the utmost inhumanity; cutting off the nose, picking out the eyes, and stabbing it through in a hundred places.' Andrew Guild, in his Latin poem, 'Bellum Bothwellianum,' records the same barbarity. 'They laid savage hands on him,' he says, 'and mutilated his manly face; having cut off his tongue, his ears, and his hands, they scattered his brains over the rough stones.' In an old ballad on the Battle of Loudon Hill—another name for the fight of Drumclog—Claverhouse's cornet and kinsman is twice made to foretell his own death:—

> ' I ken I'll ne'er come back again,
>   An' mony mae as weel as me.'

In another Covenanting poem, 'The Battle of Bothwell Brig,' Claverhouse is represented as avenging young Graham's death on the fugitives :—

> ' Haud up your hand,' then Monmouth said ;
>   ' Gie quarters to these men for me ; '
> But bloody Claver'se swore an oath,
>   His kinsman death avenged should be.

Russell, too, states that Graham was killed, and refers to the mutilation of the lifeless body, though he accounts for it in a very remarkable way. The passage is as follows : 'One Graham, that same morning in Strevan his dog was leaping upon him for meat, and he said he would give him none, but he should fill himself of the Whig's blood and flesh by night; but instead of that, his dog was seen eating his own thrapple (for he was killed), by several; and particularly James Russell after the pursuit, coming back to his dear friend James Dungel, who was severely wounded, asked at some women and men who it was ; they told that it was that Graham, and afterwards they got certain word what he said to his dog in Strevan.'

In the face of such evidence, it is hardly possible to deny the actual fact of Graham's death. Neither can it be looked upon as probable that his kinsman had no knowledge of it when he wrote his despatch. If, therefore, Claverhouse really did omit to report it amongst the other casualties, his silence is difficult to understand. But, it must be pointed out that the whole question may, after all, resolve itself into one of punctuation. The insertion of a single comma makes three persons of 'the Cornet, Mr Crafford and Captain Bleith.' A matter so utterly trifling in itself would not be deserving of notice if some of Claverhouse's irrational detractors, no less than some of his irrational apologists, had not magnified it out of all proportion.

Throughout the engagement Claverhouse made himself conspicuous by his courage, and was exposed to special

danger because of the attention which he attracted.   One
of the Covenanters, a Strathaven man, was subsequently
wont to relate that he had concealed himself behind a
hillock and fired eight shots at the leader of the royal
troops ; and it may be assumed that, in those days, want
of skill on the part of the marksman was not considered
the cause of his failure.   It is also stated by De Foe, that
William Cleland, who, in later years distinguished himself
as a soldier and rose to be Lieutenant-Colonel of the
Cameronian regiment, actually succeeded in catching hold
of Claverhouse's bridle, and that the latter had a narrow
escape of being taken prisoner.   Thanks to his coolness
and presence of mind no less than to his good fortune, he
left the field unscathed, but only when the discomfiture of
his men had become so complete as to render any effort
to rally them wholly hopeless.   Like them, he galloped
back to Strathaven ; and local tradition still points out
the spot where he shot down one of the townsmen who
endeavoured to stay him in his flight.   Some accounts
relate that on his road he had to pass the house where
the outlawed minister King had been left under guard,
when the soldiers set out for Drumclog, and that, as he
did so, his prisoner of the morning ironically invited him
to remain for the afternoon sermon.

Before the engagement, Hamilton, who had assumed the
command of the Covenanters, gave out the word that no
quarter should be given.   In spite of this, five out of seven
men who had been captured, were granted their lives and
allowed to depart.   ' This,' writes a contemporary, ' greatly
grieved Mr Hamilton, when he saw some of Babel's brats
spared, after that the Lord had delivered them into their
hands, that they might dash them against the stones.'
When he returned from the pursuit of the routed royalists,
a discussion had arisen as to the fate of the two remaining
prisoners.   Hamilton settled it, in so far at least as one
of them was concerned, by killing him on the spot.   ' None
could blame me,' he wrote in a letter of justification
published five or six years later, ' to decide the controversy ;
and I bless the Lord for it to this day.'

Wodrow gives it as 'the opinion of not a few,' that if the 'country men' had pushed their success, followed their chase, and gone straight to Glasgow that day, they might easily, with the help of the reinforcements that would have come to them on the road, as soon as their success became known, have driven out the garrison, 'and very soon made a great appearance.'

Without entering into a futile discussion as to what might have happened, it may be pointed out that the actual circumstances of the case scarcely justify so sanguine a view. When Claverhouse and his troopers rode back to Glasgow, they had no certainty that, in the flush of victory, the Covenanters would not continue the pursuit right up to the city, and endeavour to take the fullest advantage of their success. Indeed, the conduct of the royalist officers rather seems to imply that they recognised the possibility of such a course on the part of the enemy, for they caused half the men to stand to their arms all night. If, therefore, the few horsemen on the Covenanting side, who alone could possibly perform the distance of nearly thirty miles before dusk, even on a long June day, had ventured on an attack, it may be believed that they would have met with a reception calculated to make them regret their rashness.

There is no occasion to assume that any reason but that dictated by common prudence induced the foremost of the pursuers to halt at a considerable distance from Glasgow, in order to await the coming of the unmounted men, with such recruits as they might have been able to gather on the way. Statements differ as to the precise place where the greater number of them determined to stay for the night; but Wodrow is probably accurate in saying that they did not press further forward than Hamilton, and that it was from that town they resumed their march on the morrow.

In the meantime Lord Ross and his officers, Major White and Captain Graham, had not been idle. With carts, timber, and such other materials as could be hastily requisitioned, they erected four barricades in the centre of the city, and posted their men behind them to await the expected onset. At daybreak next morning, Creichton, with six dragoons, was sent out to take up his station at a small house which commanded a view of the two approaches to Glasgow, so that he might at once be able to report which of them the Covenanters decided to take. About ten o'clock he saw them advance to the place which he had been instructed to watch, and there, by a most injudicious manœuvre, divide themselves into two bodies. Of these, one, under Hamilton, marched towards the Gallowgate; whilst the other took a more circuitous road ' by the Wyndhead and College.' There may have been a vague intention of taking the military between two fires, but the movements were ill concerted, and resulted in two disjointed attacks, which were both easily repulsed.

As Creichton returned to inform Claverhouse of the enemy's dispositions, he was followed close to the heels by that detachment which was making for the Gallowgate bridge. When they reached the barricade which had been raised on that side, they were received by Claverhouse and his men with a volley which killed several, and threw the remainder into confusion. The soldiers following up this first advantage, and jumping over the carts that formed the obstruction, then charged the wavering Covenanters, and drove them out of the town. They had time to do this and to return to their original position before those of the 'country men,' who had marched round by the north, came down by the High Church and the College. These were allowed to come within pistol shot; and when the soldiers fired into them at such close range, it was with the same effect as before.

The second party was also forced to fall back. They appear to have done so in better order than Hamilton's men, for they were able to rally in a field behind the High Church, where they remained till five o'clock in the afternoon, unmolested by the soldiers, from whose sight they were concealed, and who, not knowing when they might again be attacked, and fully aware that the majority of the citizens were hostile to them, contented themselves with remaining on the defensive. Prudence prevailed with the Covenanters too, and without making any further attempt to carry the barricade, they retired to Toll Cross Moor. Finding that Claverhouse, who had been informed of the movement, had come out after them, they continued their retreat as far as Hamilton, protecting their rear so effectively with their cavalry, that Graham deemed it advisable to fall back upon Glasgow.

At Drumclog, and subsequently at Glasgow, unforeseen circumstances had imposed a leading and conspicuous part on Claverhouse. The measures which the Government was now called on to adopt for the purpose of quelling an insurrection of formidable proportions, were necessarily of such magnitude, that he naturally fell back to his own subordinate position, that of a captain of dragoons. To represent him as having incurred the displeasure of his chiefs, and as having been superseded in consequence, is contrary to fact, and wholly unfair to him. Proof is at hand that no blame was laid upon him for the defeat of Drumclog. In a letter written by the Council to Lauderdale on the 3rd of June, it was admitted that he had been overpowered by numbers; and six days later, through Lauderdale, the Chancellor conveyed the King's thanks to Lord Ross and to Claverhouse for their great diligence and care, and his assurance that he would be very mindful of their conduct on all occasions.

Creichton, who did not supply Swift with the materials for his memoirs till many years later, and who, therefore, cannot always be implicitly depended upon as regards details of minor importance, states that the morning after the attack 'the Government sent orders to Claverhouse to leave Glasgow and march to Stirling.' But Wodrow, who founds his narrative on letters which he met with in the Council Registers, and which he duly quotes, makes no special reference to Claverhouse. He simply records the fact that 'my Lord Ross and the rest of the officers of the King's forces, finding the gathering of the country people growing, and expecting every day considerable numbers to be added to them, and not reckoning themselves able to stand out a second attack, found it advisable to retire eastward.' He indicates, day by day, the marching and counter-marching of the royalist troops, and narrates all the steps that were taken to bring together a body sufficiently strong to disperse the Covenanting insurgents.

From all this it is evident that there was no room for independent action on the part of Claverhouse from the time of his leaving the West to that of his return to it with the Duke of Monmouth, who had been appointed Commander-in-Chief, and who, on the 22nd of June, encountered the Covenanters at Bothwell Bridge. In the course of the engagement which followed, no opportunity was given him of playing a prominent part. Sir Walter Scott asserts on two different occasions, that the horse were commanded by Claverhouse; and, in his well-known description of the battle, he adds the detail that 'the voice of Claverhouse was heard, even above the din of conflict, exclaiming to the soldiers—"Kill, kill—no quarter—think of Richard Grahame."' The historical truth is, that Claverhouse was simply a captain of horse, as were also the Earl of Home, and the Earl of Airlie, and that he was himself under the command of his kinsman Montrose, Colonel of the Horse Guards. Beyond stating this no accounts of the encounter make any reference to him. In so far as he is personally concerned there is no reason for recalling the incident of the fight which effectively put an end to the Covenanting insurrection. His presence at it is the single, bare fact that requires mention.

There are no official documents extant to enable us to follow Claverhouse's movements during the period immediately subsequent to Bothwell Bridge. All that has been stated with regard to his doings at this time rests on the authority of Wodrow, who himself admits, though not, it is true, for the purpose of questioning their accuracy, that the traditions embodied in his narrative were vague and uncertain. 'Everybody must see,' he says, 'that it is now almost impossible to give any tolerable view to the reader, of the spulies, depradations and violences committed by the soldiers, under such officers as at that time they had. Multitudes of instances, once flagrant are now at this distance lost; not a few of them were never distinctly known, being committed in such circumstances as upon the matter buried them.'

The order of the Privy Council, in accordance with which Claverhouse again proceeded to the Western Counties, to begin his 'circuit,' as Wodrow styles it, a few days after the engagement which had proved so disastrous to the Covenanters has disappeared. It may, however, be assumed that the powers conferred upon him were wide ; and there is no reason to suppose that he was instructed to deal leniently with those who had been in arms against the royal troops. Although no proof can be adduced in support of Wodrow's statement, that Claverhouse 'could never forgive the baffle he met with at Drumclog, and resolved to be avenged for it' ; and although it would be rash to accept, except on the very strongest evidence, the further assertion that he was one of those who solicited Monmouth 'to ruin the West Country, and burn Glasgow, Hamilton and Strathaven, to kill the prisoners, at least, considerable numbers of them, and to permit the army to plunder the western shires, who, they alleged, had countenanced the rebels,' the principles which he unhesitatingly set forth in subsequent despatches, and in accordance with which in the following July, he consented to go to London, as an envoy from the Privy Council, to represent to the King the unwisdom of adopting Monmouth's more conciliatory policy, and of granting the Covenanters favours, 'to soften the clamour that was made upon the Duke of Lauderdale's conduct,' quite justify the assumption that he fully approved of severe measures against the actual rebels, and felt neither scruple nor compunction in carrying them out.

But, when this has been admitted, it is only fair to bear in mind that there were others besides Claverhouse, and 'more bloody and barbarous than he,' engaged in the odious work of hunting down and punishing the Bothwell outlaws, and preventing their friends and sympathisers from harbouring and concealing them. If, instead of indiscriminately attributing to him every alleged act of cruelty ånd rapacity, as partisan writers have not unfrequently done, care had been taken to ascertain whether he was even indirectly concerned in it, and whether he was so circumstanced that he could prevent the perpetration of it, there can be but little doubt that the list of atrocities imputed to him at this date would assume less terrible proportions.

Nor should it be forgotten that many of the instances of severity recorded against Claverhouse, harsh as they may have been, did not go beyond the letter, or, indeed, the spirit of the law. It was his duty to yield implicit obedience to the commands of his superiors. To condemn in him that loyalty which has always been looked upon as the essential quality of a soldier, and to hold him personally responsible for carrying out with all the zeal and energy of his nature the policy of the Government to which he owed allegiance, is inconsistent and unjust.

To object that, even as a soldier, he was not bound to support a cause which he knew to be bad, is to ignore what his very enemies recognised—that he was no reckless and ungodly persecutor of religion, but, on the contrary, a man of deep convictions and of strict, almost puritanical, practice. No estimate of his character can be adequate and impartial, which does not take into account the essential fact that he was as sincere—as fanatical, if the word be insisted upon—as those whom he treated as rebels.

IV

THERE is a section of the extant correspondence of Claver-house which opens about the end of 1678 and extends through several years, and which stands in remarkable contrast with the military despatches of the same period. It consists of letters addressed to William Graham, eighth and last Earl of Menteith. That nobleman, though twice married, had no issue. His nearest male relative was his uncle, Sir James Graham, whose only children were two daughters. With a view to settling the succession to the earldom, Menteith favoured a matrimonial alliance between Lady Helen, the younger of them, and some member of the Graham family. Sir William Fraser, who discovered and published the letters, is of opinion that the first thoughts of such a scheme were suggested to the Earl by his kinsman, John Graham of Claverhouse. The following passage in the earliest letter of the extant collection, though obviously not the first of the correspondence, seems to bear out this view :—

'My Lord, as your friend and servant, I take the liberty to give you an advice, which is, that there can be nothing so advantageous for you as to settle your affairs, and establish your successor in time, for it can do you no prejudice if you come to have any children of your own body, and will be much for your quiet and comfort if you have none; for whoever you make choice of will be in place of a son. You know that Julius Cæsar had no need to regret the want of issue, having adopted Augustus, for he knew certainly that he had secured to himself a thankful and useful friend, as well as a wise successor, neither of which he could have promised himself by having children;

59

for nobody knows whether they beget wise men or fools, besides that the ties of gratitude and friendship are stronger in generous minds than those of nature.

'My Lord, I may, without being suspected of self-interest, offer some reasons to renew to you the advantage of that resolution you have taken in my favour. First, that there is nobody of my estate and of your name would confound their family in yours, and nobody in the name is able to give you those conditions, nor bring in to you so considerable an interest, besides that I will easier obtain your cousin german than any other, which brings in a great interest, and continues your family in the right line. And then, my Lord, I may say without vanity that I will do your family no dishonour, seeing there is nobody you could make choice of has toiled so much for honour as I have done, though it has been my misfortune to attain but a small share. And then, my Lord, for my respect and gratitude to your Lordship, you will have no reason to doubt of it, if you consider with what a frankness and easiness I live with all my friends.

'But, my Lord, after all this, if these reasons cannot persuade you that it is your interest to pitch on me, and if you can think on anybody that can be more proper to restore your family and contribute more to your comfort and satisfaction, make frankly choice of him, for without that you can never think of getting anything done for your family : it will be for your honour that the world see you never had thoughts of alienating your family, then they will look no more upon you as the last of so noble a race, but will consider you rather as the restorer than the ruiner, and your family rather as rising than falling ; which, as it will be the joy of our friends and relations, so it will be the confusion of our enemies.'

Claverhouse's proposal found favour with the Earl of Menteith. He wrote a very earnest letter to his 'much honorrd Unkle,' who resided in Ireland ; and formally made an offer of marriage in Claverhouse's name. He described the 'noble young gentleman' in glowing terms. He was, the Earl said, 'exceeding well accomplished with nature's gifts,'—as much so as any he knew. 'All that is noble and virtuous' might be seen in him; and as a further and not inconsiderable recommendation, it was added that he had 'a free estate upwards of six hundred pound sterling yearly of good payable rent, near by Dundee,' and also that he was 'captain of the standing troops of horse in this kingdom,' which was 'very considerable.' To crown all this, he was a Graham; and it would be 'a singular happiness' to the family to form an alliance with 'such a gentleman as he.' To persuasion the match-making Earl added something not very far removed from a menace, and concluded his letter with the following vigorous words:—

'For if ye give and bestow that young lady on any other person bot he, I sall never consent to the mariag unless it be Cleverus, whom I say again is the only person of all I know fitest and most proper to marie yor daughter.'

Claverhouse, notwithstanding the important matters that were engaging his attention at the time, was willing to go over to Ireland to prosecute his suit in person. He would not, however, presume to do so until a line from Sir James and his lady brought the assurance that he should be welcome. In the meantime, he sent a messenger, probably with letters of his own, whose delay in returning with an answer called forth the following rather desponding letter, which bears date, Dumfries, February 14th, 1679:—

'MY DEAR LORD,—I have delayed so long to give a return to your kind letter, expecting that my man should return from Ireland, that I might have given your Lordship an account of the state of my affairs; but now that I begin to despair of his coming, as I do of the success of that voyage, I would not lose this occasion of assuring your Lordship of my respects. I have received letters from my Lord Montrose, who gives me ill news, that an Irish gentleman has carried away the Lady, but it is not certain, though it be too probable. However, my Lord, it shall never alter the course of our friendship, for if, my Lord, either in history or romance, either in nature or the fancy, there be any stronger names or rarer examples of friendship

than these your Lordship does me the honour to name in
your kind and generous letter, I am resolved not only to
equal them, but surpass them, in the sincerity and firmness
of the friendship I have resolved for your Lordship. But,
my Lord, seeing it will, I hope, be more easy for me to
prove it by good deeds in time to come, than by fine words
to express it at present, I shall refer myself to time and
occasion, by which your Lordship will be fully informed
to what height I am, my dear Lord, your Lordship's most
faithful and most obedient servant,   J. GRAHAME.'

Claverhouse's fears were not without foundation. His
offer was declined. As the letter conveying Sir James's
refusal has not been preserved, it is impossible to learn
what reasons he assigned for it. The first intimation to
be found of his adverse decision occurs in a letter addressed
to him, in the following November, by his nephew, who
again approached him with a matrimonial scheme, this
time in favour of Montrose. The terms of the wholly
unromantic proposal were, that the Earldom of Menteith
should, failing heirs male, be entailed upon the young
Marquis, and that he, in return, should marry Helen
Graham, and should allow the Earl a life annuity of a
hundred and fifty pounds. Matters went so far that the
necessary charter had been submitted to the King for
signature, when Montrose broke off his engagement under
circumstances which Claverhouse details in an indignant
letter addressed from London to the Earl of Menteith,
on the 3rd of July 1680 :—

'MY LORD,—Whatever were the motives obliged your
Lordship to change your resolutions to me, yet I shall
never forget the obligations that I have to you for the
good designs you once had for me, both before my Lord
Montrose came in the play and after, in your endeavouring
to make me next in the entail, especially in so generous a
way as to do it without so much as letting me know it.
All the return I am able to make is to offer you, in that
frank and sincere way that I am known to deal with all
the world, all the service that I am capable of, were it with

the hazard or even loss of my life and fortune. Nor can I do less without ingratitude, considering what a generous and disinterested friendship I have found in your Lordship.

'And your Lordship will do me, I hope, the justice to acknowledge that I have shown all the respect to your Lordship and my Lord Montrose, in your second resolutions, that can be imagined. I never inquired at your Lordship nor him the reason of the change, nor did I complain of hard usage. Though really, my Lord, I must beg your Lordship's pardon to say that it was extremely grievous to me to be turned out of the business, after your Lordship and my Lord Montrose had engaged me in it, and had written to Ireland in my favour; and the thing that troubled me most was that I feared your Lordship had more esteem for my Lord Montrose than me, for you could have no other motive, for I am sure you have more sense than to think the offers he made you more advantageous for the standing of your family than those we were on.

'Sir James and I together would have bought in all the lands ever belonged to your predecessors, of which you would have been as much master as of those you are now in possession; and I am sorry to see so much trust in your Lordship to my Lord Montrose so ill-rewarded. If you had continued your resolutions to me, your Lordship would not have been thus in danger to have your estate rent from your family; my Lord Montrose would not have lost his reputation, as I am sorry to see he has done; Sir James would not have had so sensible an affront put upon them, if they had not refused me, and I would have been, by your Lordship's favour, this day as happy as I could wish. But, my Lord, we must all submit to the pleasure of God Almighty without murmuring, knowing that everybody will have their lot.

'My Lord, fearing I may be misrepresented to your Lordship, I think it my duty to acquaint your Lordship with my carriage since I came hither, in relation to those affairs. So soon as I came, I told Sir James how much he was obliged to you, and how sincere your designs were for the standing of your family; withal I told him that my

Lord Montrose was certainly engaged to you to marry his daughter, but that from good hands I had reason to suspect he had no design to perform it; and indeed my Lord Montrose seemed to make no address there at all in the beginning, but hearing that I went sometimes there, he feared that I might get an interest with the father, for the daughter never appeared, so observant they were to my Lord Montrose, and he thought that if I should come to make any friendship there, that when he came to be discovered I might come to be acceptable, and that your Lordship might turn the tables upon him. Wherefore he went there and entered in terms to amuse them till I should be gone, for then I was thinking every day of going away, and had been gone, had I not fallen sick. He continued thus, making them formal visits, and talking of the terms, till the time that your signature should pass; but when it came to the King's hand it was stopped upon the account of the title.

'My Lord Montrose who, during all this time had never told me anything of these affairs, nor almost had never spoken to me, by Drumeller and others, let me know that our differences proceeded from mistakes, and that if we met we might come to understand one another, upon which I went to him. After I had satisfied him of some things he complained of, he told me that the title was stopped, and asked me if I had no hand in it; for he thought it could be no other way, seeing Sir James concurred. I assured him I had not meddled in it, as before God, I had not. So he told me he would settle the title on me, if I would assist him in the passing of it. I told him that I had never any mind for the title out of the blood. He answered me, I might have Sir James's daughter and all. So I asked him how that could be. He told me he had no design there, and that to secure me the more, he had given commission to speak to my Lady Rothes about her daughter, and she had received it kindly. I asked how he would come off. He said upon their not performing the terms, and offered to serve me in it, which I refused, and would not concur. He thought to make me serve him in his designs, and break me with Sir James and his Lady: for he went and insinuated to them as if I had a design upon their daughter, and was carrying it on under hand. So soon as I heard this, I went and told my Lady Graham all. My Lord Montrose came there next day and denied it. However, they went to Windsor and secured the signature, but it was already done. They have not used me as I deserved at their hands, but my design is not to complain of them, and they had reason to trust entirely one whom your Lordship had so strongly recommended. After all came to all, that Sir James offered to perform all the conditions my Lord Montrose required, he knew not what to say, and so, being ashamed of his carriage, went away without taking leave of them; which was to finish his tricks with contempt.

'This is, my Lord, in as few words as I can, the most substantial part of that story. My Lord Montrose and some of his friends endeavoured to ruin that young lady's reputation to get an excuse for his carriage. But I made them quickly quit those designs, for there was no shadow of ground for it. And I must say she has suffered a great deal to comply with your Lordship's designs for her; and truly, my Lord, if you knew her, you would think she deserved all, and would think strange my Lord Montrose should have neglected her.

'My Lord, I know you want not the best advice of the nation, yet I think it not amiss to tell you that it is the opinion of everybody that you may recover your estate, and that you ought to come and make your case known to the King and Duke. Your family is as considerable as Caithness or Maclean, in whose standing they concern themselves highly. My Lord, you would by this means recover your affairs; you would see your cousin; and you and Sir James would understand one another, and take right measures for the standing of your family. If you let your title stand in the heirs male, your family must of necessity perish, seeing in all appearance you will outlive Sir James, and then it would come to the next brother, who has neither heirs nor estate, so that your only way will be to transfer the title to that young lady, and get the father and mother to give you the disposing of her. The Duke assures me, that if my Lord Montrose would have married her, the title should have passed, as being in the blood, and that it may be done for anybody who shall marry her with your consent.

' My Lord, if I thought your Lordship were to come up, I would wait to do you service; for your uncle is old and infirm. My Lord, I hope you will pardon this long letter, seeing it is concerning a business touches you so near, and that of a long time I have not had the happiness to entertain your Lordship. Time will show your Lordship who deserves best your friendship.

' My Lord, things fly very high here ; the indictments appear frequently against the honest Duke, and I am feared these things must break out. I am sorry for it ; but I know you, impatient of the desire of doing great things, will rejoice at this. Assure yourself, if ever there be barricades again in Glasgow, you shall not want a call ; and, my Lord, I bespeak an employment under you, which is to be your lieutenant-general, and I will assure you we will make the world talk of us. And, therefore, provide me trews, as you promised, and a good blue bonnet, and I will assure you there shall be no trews trustier than mine.

' My Lord, despond not for this disappointment, but show resolution in all you do. When my affairs go wrong, I remember that saying of Lucan, " Tam mala Pompeii quam prospera mundus adoret." One has occasion to show their vigour after a wrong step to make a nimble recovery. You have done nothing amiss, but trusted too much to honour, and thought all the world held it as sacred as you do.

' My dear Lord, I hope you will do me the honour to let me hear from you, for if there be nothing for your service here I will be in Scotland immediately, for now I am pretty well recovered. I know my Lord Montrose will endeavour to misrepresent me to your Lordship, but I hope he has forfeited his credit with you, and anything he says to you is certainly to abuse you. My Lord, I have both at home and abroad sustained the character of an honest and frank man, and defy the world to reproach me of anything. So, my Lord, as I have never failed in my respect to your Lordship, I hope you will continue that friendship for me which I have so much ambitioned. When I have the honour to see you I will say more of my inclination to serve you. I will beg the favour of a line with the first post.

'I am, my Lord, your Lordship's most faithful and humble servant,   J. GRAHAME.

'Excuse this scribbling, for I am in haste, going to Windsor, though I write two sheets.'

This long letter was followed at short intervals, by others to the same effect, full of protestations on the part of Claverhouse of his desire to serve the Earl. It would appear, however, that Menteith was not fully satisfied as to his correspondent's sincerity and disinterestedness. No direct reply to the latter's denunciation of Montrose has been preserved; but there is a communication addressed to the young Marquis himself, in which the Earl expresses himself very strongly and very plainly with regard to the 'malicious letters' too often written to him, and in which he assures him that his generous actings and noble endeavours for the standing and good of the Menteith family, vindicate to the world his Lordship's honour and reputation from the false and unjust aspersions that some unworthy and seditious persons, though they were of no mean quality, would make all men believe.

It is true that the Earl of Menteith himself had good reason for wishing to conciliate Montrose. He was not without hope that the Marquis would 'effectuate a speedy and right course and method for the relieving of the pressing debts of his poor, though ancient, family.' Moreover, he had a special favour to beg, and one which illustrates how greatly fallen from its high estate the noble house of Menteith really was. The wording and the spelling of the letter which contained it are scarcely' less remarkable than the request itself.

'My Deir Lord,—After cerious consideration with myself, I thinck most fiting and proper for me that I com to Edinburgh, God willing, agane the siting of the Parliment, the twenti-awght of the nixt month. In ceass that I should stay from the Parliment, his Royall Hyghnes might tak exceptiones, and be offended at me if I ware not at the doune sitting thairoff, and possablie might doe me much hearme in that bussines your Lordship hes in hand conserning my affaer with the King. Therfor I am fullie resolued to be at Edinburgh agane the twenty of Jwllay at fardast, wherfor I humblie intreat your Lordship to prowid and get the lene from sume Earle thair robs, fite mantle, and wellwat coats, and all things that belongs to Parliment robs. I will heave four footmen in liwra. Ther is no doubt but ther is sewerall Earles that will not ryd the Parliment. Therfor be humblye pleased to get the lene to me of sume Earle's robes onley for a day to ryde in the Parliment, and they shall be cearfulie keipt be me that none of them be spoylt, for all the robs that belonged to my grandfather was destroyed in the Einglish tyme. The last tyme when I reid the Parliment, I cearied the Secepter, and I head the lene of the deces'd Earle of Lowdian's robes, but it may be that this Earle will reid himself. I hop your Lordship will get the lene of robs to me from sume Earle or other, as also the lene of a peacable horse, because I am werie unable in both my foot and both my hands as yet. I thought good to acqwant your Lordship of this beforhand in a letter by itself. Hoping to receave tuo lines of ane answer of returne thairto from your Lordship, I pray let me know iff his Hyghnes will be Woiceroy at this Parliment, or who it is that will represent the King. I expect all the news from your Lordship, but on no termes doe not keip the bearar heirof, who is my gardner; he must surlie be at hom agan Thursdays night, so not willing to give farder trouble, I remaine wncheangablie, my deir Lord,—Your Lordship's most affectionat cousine and faithful servant,

'MENTEITH.'

The intricacy of a wooing in which there does not seem to have been an excess of love-making, is made more puzzling by a letter addressed by Isabella, wife of Sir James Graham, to the Earl of Menteith. It was written about a month later than his own obsequious epistle to Montrose; and yet it shows that at that time a match between Claverhouse and Lady Helen was again under consideration. Lady Isabella informed his Lordship that she had so far complied with his desires as to waive the propositions of two matches, though the worse of the suitors had two thousand pounds a year, besides a troop of horse, and a fair prospect of many thousands more. At the same time, she bade him bear in mind that, unless he were very willing to assist as far as he could towards the recovering of such lands as formerly belonged to his ancestors, she would decline all thoughts of matching her daughter in Scotland, where she would be a daily spectator of the ruin of the noble family she came from. Her Ladyship's very outspoken letter also referred to the dilatoriness that had so far marked the whole course of the negotiations, and let it be understood that, in her opinion, the responsibility for much of it lay with the Earl.

The delay with which Lady Graham found fault may, in its most recent phase at least, have been due to rumours and reports which had reached Menteith, to the effect that Claverhouse had spoken disparagingly of him to the Duke of Lauderdale; for the next letter in the correspondence contains an energetic, almost passionate denial of such conduct. The writer swears before Almighty God, and upon his salvation, that he has never given either a good or a bad character of the Earl to Lauderdale, and that he has not even mentioned his person or affairs to him; he declares himself ready to spend his blood in revenge of so base and cowardly an injury on the ' infamous liar ' who has traduced him, and to whom he begs his letter may be shown. From Claverhouse's special insistence on the fact that he had never cast a doubt on the Earl's capacity for affairs, it may be presumed that this was one of the points with regard to which he was charged with having 'said things.' Another letter to the Earl, written on the same day, but as a distinct and more confidential communication, suggests a suspicion that Menteith had been very near committing disastrous blunders in his efforts to urge Claverhouse's suit. In answer, doubtless, to Lady Isabella's pointed letter, the Earl had written both to her and to her daughter, and had commissioned the suitor himself to deliver these communications to the ladies. Claverhouse, however, thought it wiser to refrain from doing so, for reasons which he thus explained :—

'I have not dared to present them (the letters) because that in my Lady's letter you wished us much joy, and that we might live happy together, which looked as if you thought it a thing as good as done. I am sure my Lady, of the humour I know her to be, would have gone mad that you should think a business that concerned her so nearly, concluded before it was ever proposed to her; and in the daughter's you was pleased to tell her of my affections to her, and what I have suffered for her ; this is very galant and obliging, but I am afraid they would have miscontrued it, and it might do me prejudice ; and then in both, my Lord, you were pleased to take pains to show them almost clearly they had nothing to expect of you, and took from them all hopes which they had, by desiring them to require no more but your consent.'

The question of conditions and settlements being thus approached, Claverhouse hastens to affirm his own absolute disinterestedness. 'I will assure you,' he writes, 'I need nothing to persuade me to take that young lady. I would take her in her smock.' He is not sure, however, of such unselfish and generous treatment from the other side ; and he consequently requests the Earl to hold out hopes to them, though without binding himself in any way. 'When you say you give them your advice to the match,' he writes, 'tell them that they will not repent it, and that doing it at

your desire, you will do us any kindness you can, and look
on us as persons under your protection, and endeavour to
see us thrive—which obliges you to nothing, and yet
encourages them.'

This plain suggestion of a course which it would tax a
casuist's ingenuity to distinguish from double-dealing and
deception, is hardly creditable to Claverhouse under any
circumstances. For his sake it may be hoped that the
excuse for it lay in the fact that by this time he had really
fallen in love, and was, as he said, anxious to win the
young lady for her own sake. If such were not the case,
there would be an almost repulsive insincerity in his closing
appeal, 'For the love of God write kindly of me to them.
By getting me that young lady you make me happy.'

Two months later negotiations were still dragging on—
they had now extended, from first to last, through fully
three years, from the end of 1678 to the end of 1681.
On the 11th of December, Claverhouse again appealed to
the Earl to come to some settlement of his affairs, either
one way or the other, for, in the meantime, his own age
was slipping away, and he was losing other occasions, as
he supposed the young lady also was doing. The Grahams,
he feared, had gone back to Ireland; and, if it were so, he
proposed to invite them to come over to his house in
Galloway. But it would be necessary to offer something
definite to induce them to do so, for, 'my Lady Graham
was a very cunning woman, and certainly would write back
that she would be unwilling to come so far upon uncer-
tainties.' He therefore further suggested that the Earl should
communicate directly with her Ladyship. That 'they would
take it much more kindly, and be far the readier to comply'
was the reason urged for this. But another was hinted.
Claverhouse was ashamed to write, not knowing what to
say, seeing that after all he had promised on Menteith's
behalf, his Lordship had not yet come to a final decision.

Claverhouse's letter does not appear to have produced
any effect. As late as the beginning of March 1682,
matters were still in the same unsettled and unsatisfactory
state. The Earl had not yet resolved on any decisive

action, and was doubtless endeavouring to make a bargain as favourable as possible to himself, when he received a short but urgent letter from Claverhouse. It asked for an early meeting, and indicated the reason for it in these words : ' I have had one in Ireland whom I shall bring along with me, and you shall know all. Send nobody to Ireland ; but take no new measures till I can see you.'

There are no letters from Claverhouse relative to subsequent negotiations. It appears from other documents, however, that Sir James Graham had come to believe in the existence of a plot between the two suitors, to get the better of both him and the Earl. Everything, he declared, had been contrived by the hand of Claverhouse ; and it was his ambitious desire to make himself the head of their ancient family that had brought them all the trouble of my Lord Montrose's business. There was, he asserted, an agreement that Montrose should use his interest with the Earl for a settlement of his honours and estates upon Claverhouse, who, on his side, had bound himself to make over the estates privately to Montrose. The letter setting all this forth in tones of the bitterest resentment was written from Drogheda in March 1683. Before that, however, Lady Helen had made further matrimonial arrangements impossible. She had married Captain Rawdon, son of Sir George Rawdon, and nephew, as well as heir apparent to the Earl of Conway. And so an Irish gentleman, who was possibly no myth when Montrose wrote about him four years earlier, carried away the lady.

V

MATTERS CIVIL, MILITARY AND MATRIMONIAL

THE letters which enable us to trace the course of Claver-house's matrimonial negotiations are also the documents upon which we have mainly to depend for our knowledge of his movements during the period immediately sub-sequent to the 'circuit' which he made in the south-western counties after the Battle of Bothwell Bridge. From these we learn that he was in London during the summer of 1680; and a letter from Charles Maitland of Hatton to Queensberry, suggests a probable motive for the journey to town. 'Claverhouse's commission as to the rebels' goods,' he wrote, 'is recalled by the Council; so your man will have room for his payment; that ye need not fear.' This measure, with which, to judge from the tenor of Maitland's remarks, Queensberry was not improbably connected, appears to have followed upon a charge of misappropria-tion of public monies, brought against Claverhouse by the Treasurer, and intended to supply an excuse for preventing him from entering into possession of the forfeited estate of Patrick Macdowall of Freugh, bestowed upon him by royal grant in consideration of 'his good and faithful services.' It is warrantable to suppose that the immediate object of his journey to London was to appeal from the Council's decision to the King himself. In any case, there is evidence that he availed himself of his stay in the English capital to bring the matter before his sovereign, and to plead his cause in person. The result may be gathered from a letter addressed by Charles to the Lords Commis-sioners of the Treasury, on the 26th of February 1681. 'As to what you have represented concerning Claverhouse, particularly in reference to the commission granted by you unto him for uplifting and sequestrating not only the rents, duties, and movables belonging to Freugh, but of all the rebels in Wigtownshire who have been in the rebellion, whereof you say he hath made no account yet, we have spoke to him about it, and he doth positively assert, that, while he was in Scotland, he received not one farthing upon that account, and that if anything have since been recovered by those whom in his absence he hath entrusted with the execution of that commission, he believes it to be so inconsiderable as it will not much exceed the charges that must necessarily be laid out in that affair. However, we do expect that he will meet with no worse usage from you, upon that occasion than others to whom you have granted the like commissions.' The letter also conveyed his Majesty's 'express pleasure' that the Commissioners should remove the stop that was put upon the gift of forfeiture, and should cause the same to be passed in the Exchequer at their very next meeting.

In October 1681, also, Claverhouse was in London; and though there is nothing to show whether his stay there had been continuous, the fact that there is no record of his doings in Scotland during the interval, may be taken as negative, yet strong, evidence of his absence from the country. There is a curious document to prove that, on the 26th of the next month he crossed the Firth of Forth from Burntisland to Leith. It is a poem entitled 'The Tempest,' and written by Alexander Tyler, the minister of Kinnettles, who describes it as 'being an account of a dangerous passage from Burntisland to Leith in a boat called the *Blessing*, in company of Claverhouse, several gentlewomen, ministers and a whole throng of common passengers upon the 26th of November 1681.' On the 11th of the following month, Claverhouse dates a letter from Edinburgh; and, from that time, his activity and his influence again begin to be felt.

The Earl of Queensberry, writing from Sanquhar to Lord Haddo on the 2nd of January 1682, reports that in his part of the country all is peaceable, 'save only that in the heads of Galloway some rebels meet.' Their numbers being inconsiderable, and their business 'only to drink and quarrel,' neither Church nor State need, in his judgment, fear them; still, he is of opinion that 'the sooner garrisons be placed, and a competent party sent with Claverhouse for scouring that part of the country, the better.' 'Besides,' he adds, 'I'm told field-conventicles continue in Annandale and Galloway, but all will certainly evanish upon Claverhouse's arrival, as I have often told.' It would appear from this, that Captain Graham had returned to Scotland for a special and definite purpose; and this view is borne out by his appointment on the 31st of January to be heritable sheriff of Wigtownshire, in the place of Sir Andrew Agnew of Lochnaw, and heritable bailie of the regality of Tongland, instead of Viscount Kenmure, both the former possessors having been deprived of their commissions in consequence of their refusal to take the prescribed test. In terms of his appointment, Claverhouse was to have jurisdiction within the shire of Dumfries and stewartries of Kirkcudbright and Annandale; but, with regard to these districts, it was specially provided that the powers conferred upon him were in no way to be prejudicial to the rights of the heritable sheriff or steward, and that he was 'only to proceed and do justice,' when he was 'the first attacher,' that is to say, only in cases with regard to which no legal proceedings had already been taken.

Claverhouse had not long assumed his new duties before he discovered that the 'rebels' and 'conventiclers' were not the only people with whom he had to deal, and that a task far more difficult than hunting them down or scattering their meetings would be to expose the connivance of some of the leading families, and to check the disorders arising from it. As early as the 5th of March, in a letter to Queensberry, he wrote, 'Here, in the shire, I find the lairds all following the example of a late great man, and still a considerable heritor among them, which is, to live regularly themselves, but have their houses constant haunts of rebels and intercommuned persons, and have their children baptized by the same; and then lay all the blame on their wives; condemning them and swearing they cannot help what is done in their absence. But I am resolved this jest shall pass no longer here; for it is laughing and fooling the Government; and it will be more of consequence to punish one considerable laird, than a hundred little bodies. Besides, it is juster; because these only sin by the example of those.'

At the date of this communication, Claverhouse had already begun to carry out the policy to which it referred; and a letter written four days earlier supplies important details as to the course which he had adopted. 'The way that I see taken in other places, is to put laws severely, against great and small, in execution, which is very just; but what effects does that produce, but more to exasperate and alienate the hearts of the whole body of the people? For it renders three desperate where it gains one; and your Lordship knows that in the greatest crimes it is thought wisest to pardon the multitude and punish the ringleaders, where the number of the guilty is great, as in this case of whole countries. Wherefore, I have taken another course here. I have called two or three parishes together at one church, and after intimating to them the power I have, I read them a libel narrating all the Acts of Parliament against the fanatics; whereby I made them sensible how much they were in the King's reverence, and assured them he was relenting nothing of his former severity against dissenters, nor care of maintaining the established government; as they might see by his doubling the fines in the late Act of Parliament; and, in the end, told them that the King had no design to ruin any of his subjects he could reclaim, nor I to enrich myself by their crimes; and, therefore, any who would resolve to conform, and live regularly, might expect favour; excepting only resetters and ringleaders. Upon this, on Sunday last, there was about three hundred people at Kirkcudbright church; some that for seven years before had never been there. So that I do expect that within a short time I could bring two parts of three to the church.'

But though there seemed to be some hope of influencing the people, if they were left to themselves, Claverhouse was fully alive to the fact that it was vain to think of any settlement so long as their irreconcilable ministers were able to exercise their influence. No sooner was he gone, than they came in, he said, and all repented and fell back to their old ways. With a view to remedying this, he strongly and repeatedly urged the necessity of having a constant force of dragoons in garrison ; and, in the meantime, he took vigorous measures to carry out the work entrusted to him. To quote his own summary of a report presented by him to the Committee of the Privy Council, 'The first work he did, was to provide magazines of corn and straw in every part of the country, that he might with conveniency go with the whole party wherever the King's service required ; and, running from one place to another, nobody could know where to surprise him ; and in the meantime quartered on the rebels, and endeavoured to destroy them by eating up their provisions, but that they quickly perceived the design, and sowed their corns on untilled ground. After which he fell in search of the rebels ; played them hotly with parties ; so that there were several taken, many fled the country, and all were dung from their haunts ; and then rifled so their houses, ruined their goods, and imprisoned their servants, that their wives and children were brought to starving ; which forced them to have recourse to the safe conduct ; and made them glad to renounce their principles, declare Bothwell Bridge an unlawful rebellion, swear never to rise in arms against the King, his heirs and successors, or any having commission or authority from him, upon any pretext whatsomever, and promise to live orderly hereafter.'

Three months of this repressive and coercive policy produced results which Claverhouse himself declared to be beyond his expectation. Writing to Queensberry, on the 1st of April 1682, he said, 'I am very happy in this business of this country, and I hope the Duke will have no reason to blame your Lordship for advising him to send the forces hither. For this country now is in perfect peace: all who were in the rebellion are either seized, gone out of the country, or treating their peace; and they have already so conformed, as to going to the church, that it is beyond my expectation. In Dumfries, not only almost all the men are come, but the women have given obedience; and Irongray, Welsh's own parish, have for the most part conformed; and so it is over all the country. So that, if I be suffered to stay any time here, I do expect to see this the best settled part of the Kingdom on this side the Tay. And if those dragoons were fixed which I wrote your Lordship about, I might promise for the continuance of it.

'Your Lordship's friends here are very assisting to me in all this work; and it does not contribute a little to the progress of it, that the world knows I have your Lordship's countenance in what I do. All this is done without having received a farthing money, either in Nithsdale, Annandale, or Kirkcudbright; or imprisoned anybody. But, in end, there will be need to make examples of the stubborn that will not comply. Nor will there be any danger in this after we have gained the great body of the people; to whom I am become acceptable enough; having passed all bygones, upon bonds of regular carriage hereafter.'

The measures adopted by Claverhouse met with the fullest approval of the Government, and the results achieved through them were deemed so satisfactory as to call for special recognition. Wodrow states that on the 15th of May, 'Claverhouse got the Council's thanks for his diligence in executing his commission in Galloway.'

Further evidence of the favour in which Claverhouse was held is afforded by the instructions given by the Council to General Dalziel, in view of the military visitation of the shires of Lanark and of Ayr, which he was appointed to hold. He is directed 'to repair to the town of Ayr, and there to meet with the Earl of Dumfries, and the Commissioners of that shire, where the laird of Claverhouse is to be present, and there to confer with them anent the security of that shire.' After having complied with this, he is to return to the shire of Lanark, and the laird of Claverhouse with him, 'and there to consider what further is necessary to be done, as to the settling of the peace of both these shires.' Finally, when these matters have been fully considered and discussed by them, he and Claverhouse 'are to come in with all possible diligence, and give an account to the Lord Chancellor' of their procedure, 'to be communicated to his Majesty's Privy Council.'

When Claverhouse was returning from Edinburgh to Galloway, at the conclusion of this mission, there occurred an incident which must have convinced him that, even if, as he said, he had become acceptable enough to the great body of the people, there was a remnant of desperate men, whom his repressive measures had only inspired with a still fiercer hatred of him. His own account of it is contained in a letter to Queensberry, to whom he says: "I thought to have waited on your Lordship before this, but I was stayed at Edinburgh two days beyond what I designed, which has proved favourable for me. Yesterday when I came at the Bille, I was certainly informed that several parties of Whigs in arms, to the number of six or seven score, were gone from thence but six hours before. They came from Clydesdale upon Monday night, and passed Tweed at the Bille, going towards Teviotdale, but went not above three miles farther that way. They stayed thereabout, divided in small parties, most all on foot, Tuesday, Wednesday, and Thursday, till Friday morning, when they passed the hills towards Clydesdale. Some say they had a meeting with Teviotdale folks; others would make me believe that they had a mind for me. They did ask, in several places, what they heard of me, and told they were sure my troop was far in, in Galloway. Others say they were flying the West for fear of the diligence the gentry is designed to use for their discovery. I could believe this, were they not returned. I spoke with the minister, and several other people in whose houses they were; but he kept out of the way. They did no prejudice in his house, further than meat and drink. They gave no where that I could learn any account of their design there; only, I heard they said they were seeking the enemies of God, and inquired roughly if anybody there kept the church. The country keeps up this business. I heard nothing of it till I was within two miles of the Bille, and that was from a gentleman on the road, who had heard it at a burial the day before. There was a dragoon all Tuesday night at the change-house at the Bille, and the master of the house confessed to me he let him know nothing of it. They pretend it is for fear of bringing trouble to the country. I sent from the Bille an express to acquaint my Lord Chancellor with it; for I thought it fit the quarters should be advertised not to be too secure, when these rogues had the impudence to go about so.'

Queensberry was as fully convinced as Claverhouse that there had been a plot, which the unforeseen delay in Edinburgh had alone prevented from being put to execution. Writing to the Chancellor a few days later, he said: 'I doubt not but your Lordship has full account of Clavers' re-encounter at the Bille. It was good he did not come a day sooner; for certainly their design was against him.'

In the course of the year 1682, the jealousy aroused by Claverhouse's appointment as Sheriff-Principal of Wigtown-shire, and by the special power bestowed upon him to hold criminal courts, culminated in an open quarrel between him and the family of Stair, of which the head was Sir James Dalrymple, who, but a short time previously, had fallen into disgrace, and had been virtually deposed from his office of President of the Court of Session, for not conforming with the Test Act. According to the summary given of the case by Fountainhall, who was one of the counsel for the Stair family, Captain Graham of Claverhouse having imprisoned some of the Dalrymples' tenants in Galloway for absenting themselves from the parish church and attending conventicles, Sir John, the ex-president's son, took up the matter, and presented a bill of suspension to the Privy Council, alleging that he, as heritable Bailie of the Regality of Glenluce, within which the peasants lived, had already taken cognizance of their case; and that Claverhouse, not being the first attacher, was precluded by the limitations and restrictions of his commission, from taking action in the matter, and had no claim to the 'casualities and emoluments of the fine.'

Claverhouse replied that it was he who had first cited the offenders, and that Sir John's action was collusive. When the matter was first brought before the Privy Council, it was ordained that the imprisoned tenants should be set at liberty, after consigning their fines, which Fountainhall denounces as 'most exorbitant,' into the hands of the clerk. The point of jurisdiction was reserved; but in the meantime, the Council administered a reprimand to the Dalrymples, and told them in very plain terms, that 'heritable Bailies and Sheriffs who were negligent themselves in putting the laws in execution, should not offer to compete with the Sheriffs commissioned and put in by the Council, who executed vigorously the King's law.'

But it was not Claverhouse's intention that his opponent should escape so easily. He met the charges made against him with a bill of complaint, in which the gravest accusations followed each other in overwhelming array. The leading counts in the indictment bore that Sir John Dalrymple had weakened the hands of the Government in the county of Galloway, by traversing and opposing the commission which the King's Council had given Claverhouse; that he had done his utmost to stir up the people to a dislike of the King's forces there; that he kept disloyal and disaffected persons to be bailies and clerks in his regality, and had not administered the test to them till long after January 1682, contrary to the Act of Parliament; that he had imposed on delinquents mock fines, not the fiftieth or sixtieth part of what the law required, for the sole purpose of anticipating and forestalling Claverhouse; that he and his father had offered Claverhouse a bribe of £150 sterling, out of the fines, to connive at the irregularities of his mother, Lady Stair, of his sisters, and of others; that he had laughed insolently at the proclamation of a court, made

F

by Claverhouse, and had ordered his tenants not to
attend it; that he had traduced and defamed Claverhouse
to the Privy Council; and that he had accused him of
cheating the King's Treasury, by exacting fines and not
accounting for them.

When Sir John Dalrymple's answers to these charges
had been read, the Chancellor gave some indication of
the temper and feeling of the Council by reproving him
'for his tart reflections on Claverhouse's ingenuity,' and
by denying his right to adduce witnesses, whilst, on the
other side, Claverhouse was allowed to call whom he
chose, in support of the charges brought by him against
Sir John.   Fountainhall states that 'there was much
transport, flame, and humour in this cause;' and he
mentions that, at one phase of the proceedings, when
Dalrymple alleged that the people of Galloway had turned
orderly and regular, Claverhouse, alluding to the latest
Edinburgh novelty of the time, replied that there were
as many elephants and crocodiles in Galloway as loyal
subjects.   According to Sir John himself, Claverhouse
went much further than a direct denial of his opponents
assertions, and, in the presence of the Committee of
Council appointed to examine witnesses, threatened to
give him a box in the ear.

As might have been foreseen from the tone and tenor
of the whole proceedings, the judgment of the Council,
pronounced on the 12th of February 1683, was a complete
triumph for Claverhouse.   Not only was it found that he
had done nothing but what was legal and consonant with
his commission and instructions; but, in addition to that,
the Chancellor complimented him, and, expressing wonder
that he, not being a lawyer, had walked so warily in so
irregular a country, conveyed to him the Council's thanks,
as an encouragement.   With regard to Sir John Dalrymple,
on the other hand, the finding of the Council, set forth
under five specific heads, was, generally, to the effect that
he had exceeded his commission, weakened the authority
of the King and of the Council, and interfered with the
due administration of the law.   In punishment of his

conduct, he was deprived of his jurisdiction and office, as bailie of the regality of Glenluce, and fined in the sum of £500 sterling. Further, it was ordered that he should be submitted prisoner in the Castle of Edinburgh, and detained there, not merely till the money was paid, but during the Council's pleasure. His incarceration was not, however, of long duration. He was liberated on the 20th of the same month, after paying the fine, acknowledging his rashness, and craving the Council's pardon.

Whilst the matter between Claverhouse and Dalrymple was still pending, neither the Duke of York nor the King appears to have felt conscious of any impropriety in giving expression to his personal sentiments and sympathy. The former, writing to Queensberry at the beginning of December, said: 'I am absolutely of your mind as to Claverhouse; and think his presence more necessary in Galloway than anywhere else; for he need not fear anything Stairs can say of him, his Majesty being so well satisfied with him.' On the 25th of the same month, Charles, to show his appreciation of Claverhouse's 'loyalty, courage, and good conduct,' appointed him to be Colonel of a regiment of horse, which was formed for his special benefit, and also gave him the captaincy of a troop in the same regiment.

Shortly after his promotion Claverhouse undertook a journey to the English court, partly on public business, as the bearer of despatches from the Council, and partly as a private suitor, not only on his own behalf but also in the interest of others who had not been slow to recognise the favour in which he stood, and were anxious to avail themselves of his influence. At this time, the Committee which, in June 1682, had been appointed to investigate the charges of peculation and malversation brought against Charles Maitland of Hatton, younger brother and heir presumptive to the Duke of Lauderdale, whom the family influence had raised to the responsible position of General of the Scottish mint, had not yet presented its report; but there existed no doubt that the decision would prove adverse to Hatton, who had, in the meantime, become Earl of Lauderdale, and greedy suitors were already preparing to put forward their claims to a share of the spoils which the ruin of the family would place at the King's disposal. Amongst these were Queensberry who, though but lately raised to a marquisate, already aspired to a dukedom, and Gordon of Haddo, who was anxious to obtain a grant of money, either a thousand pounds sterling a year, or twenty thousand pounds sterling, which were thought to be the equivalent, to enable him to maintain the double dignity of High Chancellor and of Earl of Aberdeen recently conferred upon him.

Claverhouse, too, meant to avail himself of the opportunity thus offered him, for the purpose of adding to his own estates in Forfarshire the neighbouring lands of Dudhope, and of obtaining the constabulary of Dundee. The main object of his visit to England was to look after these several interests; and the letters written by him from Newmarket, where the King and the Duke of York were staying at the time, give his correspondents in Scotland a full and detailed account of the manner in which he discharged his commission, in the intervals of 'cock-fighting and courses.'

When he returned to Scotland, about the middle of May 1683, he was able to convey to those concerned satisfactory assurances, which the sequel justified, as to the success of the extensive job which they had planned between them. He had been preceded by a royal letter in which Charles informed his 'right trusty and right well-beloved cousins and counsellors' of his desire that Colonel John Graham of Claverhouse, in consideration of his loyalty, abilities, and eminent services, should be received and admitted a Privy Councillor. Claverhouse was accordingly sworn in, on the 22nd of the month, and at once took an important part in carrying out the further punitive measures which had been determined upon during his stay at the English Court, and of which he was, in all probability, the instigator.

More than twelve months earlier, on the report that an 'indulgence' was to be granted, he had protested to Queensberry against such a course, and had expressed a hope that nobody would be so mad as to advise it. There is every reason to suppose that, as soon as the opportunity occurred, he laid before the King opinions consonant with this, and was directly instrumental in the appointment of a Circuit Court of Justiciary for the enforcement of the Test Act.   It was his views which the royal proclamation embodied in the statement that the indemnities, indulgences, and other favours granted to the fanatic and disaffected party had hitherto produced no other effect than to encourage them to further disorders and to embolden them to abuse the royal goodness; it was his conviction to which it gave utterance in the assertion that neither difference in religion, nor tenderness of conscience, but merely principles of disloyalty and disaffection to the Government moved them to disturb the quiet of the King's reign and the peace of his kingdom; and it was his experience of the evasions and subterfuges used by them which dictated the steps to be taken, not only for the punishment of obstinate recusants, but also for the encouragement of the well-intentioned whom circumstances might hitherto have prevented from formally signifying their submission and promising obedience.

The first sitting of the Circuit Court of Justiciary was to be held at Stirling on the 5th of June.   A few days previously, the Privy Council issued an order that Colonel John Graham of Claverhouse should go along with the Justices during their whole progress in the Justice Air, and should command the forces in every place visited by them, with the exception of Glasgow and Stirling, where it was supposed the Lieutenant-General would be present.   To this circumstance we owe it that a report of the only case in which sentence of death was pronounced, can be given in his own words.   It is contained in a letter to the Lord Chancellor, and is deserving of notice, not merely on account of the facts which it relates, for those may be gathered from other documents, but also because of the sentiments and principles which the writer found opportunity to express in it, and which help us to understand the spirit by which Claverhouse was actuated, and the view which he took of both duty and expediency in carrying out the law.

As a brief recapitulation of Boog's case, the writer says ·
'He was actually in the rebellion; continued in that state
for four years; and now comes in with a false, sham
certificate to fool the judges. For, being desired to give
his oath that he had taken the bond, he positively refused.
Being asked if Bothwell Bridge was a rebellion, refused to
declare it so. Or the Bishop's murder, a murder. And
positively refused, in the face of the Court, the benefit of
the King's indemnity by taking the Test. Upon which
the Judges, moved by the outcry of all the bystanders, as
by their conviction of the wickedness of the man, referred
the matter to the knowledge of an inquest, who brought
him in guilty. After which, he begged to acknowledge his
folly; and offered to take the Test, with the old gloss,—
"as far as it consisted with the Protestant religion, and the
glory of God." And after that was refused him, offered in
end to take it any way. By all which it clearly appears,
that he would do anything to save his life, but nothing to
be reconciled to Government.'

After having thus summarised the heads of the case,
Claverhouse proceeds to justify the action of the Government in not allowing men to take the Test after they were
condemned. All casuists agree, he says, that an oath
imposed where the alternative is hanging cannot in any
way be binding; and it may consequently be supposed
that they who refused it when they had the freedom of
choice, and took it after being condemned, did it only
because they thought themselves not bound to keep it.
In point of prudence, too, he argues, such leniency would
be misplaced and pernicious; it would leave it in the
power of the disaffected to continue all their tricks up to
the very last day fixed for taking benefit of the indemnity,
and then, if they should be apprehended and condemned,
enable them to escape the punishment of their treason by
taking the Test. Against this he protests as turning the
whole thing into ridicule; 'for great clemency has, and
ought to be, shown to people that are sincerely resolved
to be reclaimed, but the King's indemnity should not be
forced on villains.' As to the effect which severity in

Boog's case might produce, Claverhouse scouts the idea that it would deter others from 'coming in'; and in support of his opinion to the contrary, he points to the actual fact that twenty have taken the Test since the man was condemned, and that the 'terror of his usage' is generally looked upon as likely to induce many more to submit.

Referring to the rescue of a prisoner, which had recently been effected by a party of armed men, and in the course of which one of the King's guards had been killed—a crime for which Wharry and Smith were subsequently executed in Glasgow and hung in chains near Inchbelly-bridge, between Kirkintilloch and Kilsyth, where their 'monument' may still be seen—Claverhouse continues, 'If this man should not be hanged, they would take advantage, that they have disappointed us by rescuing the other, and give us such apprehensions that we durst not venture on this.' Then he gives expression to a sentiment which should never be lost sight of in forming an estimate of his character and conduct: 'I am as sorry to see a man die, even a Whig, as any of themselves. But when one dies justly, for his own faults, and may save a hundred to fall in the like, I have no scruple.'

At the beginning of July 1683, Claverhouse returned to Edinburgh. For the next ten months his labours mainly consisted in attendance at the meetings of the Privy Council, and do not bring him specially into prominence. Towards the close of the comparatively quiet period he again appears in the character of a suitor. On this occasion, his matrimonial plans met with more success than those of which Lady Helen Graham had been the object. By what may seem a singular freak of fate, Jean, youngest daughter of the late Lord Cochrane, the lady on whom he had bestowed his affections, belonged to a family of strong Covenanting sympathies. Her father had, in the earlier days of the religious troubles, refused the Bond, and protested against the illegality of the clause which obliged masters to answer for their servants' attendance at church. Her mother, a Kennedy by birth, professed the stern and uncompromising Presbyterianism of her house. Her grandfather, Lord Dundonald, had been the subject of an inquisition for keeping a chaplain who prayed God to bless the rebels in the West with success. And her uncle, Sir John Cochrane, was an outlawed rebel and a suspected traitor.

The circumstances of Claverhouse's wooing were not overlooked by his enemies and ill-wishers. Amongst them was the Duke of Hamilton, whose professed loyalty does not appear to have placed him above suspicion, and whose daughter, Lady Susannah, was at this very time sought in marriage by Lord Cochrane, Claverhouse's prospective brother-in-law. This coincidence afforded the Duke an opportunity of which he ingeniously availed himself to direct attention to the nature of the alliance contemplated by Claverhouse. The way in which he did so is indicated by the following passage from a letter addressed by the latter to Queensberry. Referring to his intended marriage, he says: 'My Lord Duke Hamilton has refused to treat of giving his daughter to my Lord Cochrane till he should have the King and the Duke's leave. This, I understand, has been advised him, to load me. Wherefore I have written to the Duke, and told him that I would have done it sooner, had I not judged it presumption in me to trouble his Highness with my little concerns; and that I looked upon myself as a cleanser, that may cure others by coming amongst them, but cannot be infected by any plague of Presbytery; besides, that I saw nothing singular in my Lord Dundonald's case, save that he has but one rebel on his land for ten that the rest of the lords and lairds of the South and West have on theirs; and that he is willing to depone that he knew not of there being such. The Duke is juster than to charge my Lord Dundonald with Sir John's crimes. He is a madman, and let him perish; they deserve to be damned would own him. The Duke knows what it is to have sons and nephews that follow not advice.

'I have taken pains to know the state of the country's guilt as to reset; and if I make it not appear that my Lord Dundonald is one of the clearest of all that country, and can hardly be reached in law, I am content to pay his fine.

I never pleaded for any, nor shall I hereafter. But I must say I think it hard that no regard is had to a man in so favourable circumstances—I mean considering others— upon my account, and that nobody offered to meddle with him till they heard I was likely to be concerned in him.' After further comments and protests in this tone of suppressed indignation, he concludes his letter with the following emphatic words: 'Whatever come of this, let not my enemies misrepresent me. They may abuse the Duke for a time, and hardly. But, or long, I will, in despite of them, let the world see that it is not in the power of love, nor any other folly, to alter my loyalty.'

There is a remarkable proof of the annoyance which Claverhouse felt at the attacks directed against him, and, perhaps, also of his secret consciousness that if the political position of his intended bride's family did not wholly justify them, it at least supplied that element of partial truth which makes slander doubly dangerous. On the same day he wrote another letter to Queensberry, and dealt once more and at considerable length with his approaching marriage. After again expressing his opinion as to the real motive and meaning of Hamilton's ostentatious scruples, and repeating the assurance that he was proof against the infection of Presbyterianism, he asserted, if not the absolute at least the comparative, loyalty of the Cochrane family, in which he saw very little but might be easily rubbed off, and added what was even more important, an emphatic declaration of the soundness of Lady Jean's own sentiments. 'And for the young lady herself, I shall answer for her. Had she not been right principled, she would never in despite of her mother and relations, have made choice of a persecutor, as they call me. So, whoever thinks to misrepresent me on that head, will find themselves mistaken. For both in the King's and the Church's cause, drive as fast as they think fit, they will never see me behind. However, my Lord, malice sometimes carries things far; so I must beg your Lordship will defend me if you find anything of this kind stirring.'

This was written on the 19th of May 1684. On the

9th of the following month, the marriage contract between Colonel John Graham of Claverhouse and Lady Jean Cochrane was signed in Paisley. The bride's mother had, apparently, proved relentless in her opposition to the 'persecutor.' Her signature does not appear on the document.

The lady's dowry consisted of forty thousand merks— rather more than two thousand pounds sterling. Her jointure was fixed at five thousand merks, or about two hundred and seventy-six pounds yearly. As heritable security for it, the bridegroom's lands and houses were set forth in imposing array. Amongst them was included the estate of Dudhope which, with the Constabulary of Dundee, had come into Claverhouse's possession a few months earlier, after prolonged litigation, and in spite of a private bargain which Aberdeen and Lauderdale had made between them, and which but for the direct interposition of the King's authority, would have prevented his acquiring the long coveted lands.

Whilst Claverhouse was in Paisley, events were leading up to a sudden and dramatic interruption of the bridal festivities. On Sunday, the 8th of June, that is, the day before that upon which the marriage contract was signed, General Dalziel, the commander of the forces in Glasgow, received information, as he was 'at the forenoon's sermon,' that a conventicle was being held near the Black Loch, a small lake in Renfrewshire, about eight miles south-east of Paisley. He at once sent out forty men, of whom twenty were dragoons, under the command of Lieutenant-Colonel Winrhame. They were informed that a party of about a hundred, mostly men armed with guns and swords, had assembled at Drumlech-hill, and had thence proceeded through the moors, in a south-westerly direction. But, though traces of them were found at Allanton, at Cambus-nethan, and at Crossford, where they passed the water, the nature of the country made it impossible to come up with them. After marching all night in fruitless pursuit, Winrhame returned to Glasgow on the Monday with his wearied men.

On the previous Saturday, Claverhouse had informed

Dalziel of his departure for Paisley, so that there might be no delay in conveying orders to him, if he were required for special duty. Possibly out of consideration for the bridegroom, it was not to him, but to Lord Ross, who was one of the wedding guests, and had acted as witness for his brother-officer the day before, that, on the Tuesday morning, the General sent information of what had taken place.

When the purport of the letter was communicated to Claverhouse, he had no hesitation as to his own course of action. With a growl at the 'dogs,' who 'might have let Tuesday pass,' and a vow that he would, some time or other, be revenged on them for 'the unseasonable trouble' they were causing him, he made hasty preparation, and set out on the rebels' track. Tuesday night and Wednesday all day he scoured the country, leaving 'no den, no knowe, no moss, no hill unsearched.' Beyond catching sight of two men, who were running to the hills, but who, on account of the marshy nature of the ground, could not be overtaken he was not more successful than Winrhame had been. On reaching Strathaven, he decided to ride back to Paisley, and gave over the command to Colonel Buchan, with instructions to follow more leisurely and, on his march, to search the skirts of the hills and moors on the Clydesdale side.

On the Friday morning Buchan sent his superior officer a report of the stirring incidents of the previous day. After Claverhouse had left him, he had met a man from whom he learnt that there were numbers of rebels in arms in the heart of the hills, on the Clydesdale side, and who gave him a description of the two leaders—one a lusty, black, one-eyed man, with a velvet cap; the other a good-like man, who wore a grey hat. Buchan at once made for the place which had been indicated. On the way to it, a party of foot, that he had sent out on his right, accidentally came upon the armed Covenanters. Four soldiers, who formed a kind of advance-guard, were fired on by seven men that started up suddenly, out of a glen, and one of them was wounded. The other three, after discharging their pieces without effect at their assailants, thought it safer not to venture in pursuit over the treacherous ground.

Hastening back, they informed their colonel of the encounter; but, though Buchan made all possible diligence,
he could not succeed in even catching sight of the fugitives.
He could only learn that they had made for Cumnock, and
he himself proceeded with all speed in the same direction,
in the hope of preventing their passing into Galloway.

By noon that same Friday, Claverhouse had again taken
a hurried leave of his bride, and was on the road to
Ayrshire. From that point his movements may best be
narrated in his own terse words: 'I went immediately to
Mauchline, and from this to Cumnock, where we learned
that on Thursday night they had passed at the bog-head,
near Airdsmoss, and were then only fifty-nine in arms.
They were running in great haste, barefooted many of
them, and taking horses in some places, to help them
forward. We heard they went from that to a place called
the Hakhill, within two miles of Cumnock, and from that
to the Gap, which goes to the hills lying betwixt the
Sanquhar and Moffat. But we could never hear more of
them. I sent on Friday night for my troop from Dumfries,
and ordered them to march by the Sanquhar to the
Muirkirk, to the Ploughlands, and so to Straven. I sent
for Captain Strachan's troop from the Glenkens, and
ordered him to march to the old castle of Cumnock, down
to the Lorne, and through the country to Kilbride, leaving
Mauchline and Newmills on his left, and Loudon-hill on
his right. By this means they scoured this country, and
secured the passages that way.

'Colonel Buchan marched with the foot and dragoons
some miles on the right of my troop, and I, with the Guards
and my Lord Ross and his troop up by the (Shaire?).
We were at the head of Douglas. We were round and
over Cairntable. We were at Greenock-head, Cummer-
head, and through all the moors, mosses, hills, glens, woods;
and spread in small parties, and ranged as if we had been
at hunting, and down to Blackwood, but could learn nothing
of those rogues. So the troops being extremely harassed
with marching so much on grounds never trod on before, I
have sent them with Colonel Buchan to rest at Dalmel-

lington, till we see where these rogues will start up. We examined all on oath, and offered money, and threatened terribly, for intelligence, but we could learn no more.'

No further information is available as to the result of Claverhouse's search. That a number of people residing in the district were apprehended about this time, however, appears from the fact that the next recorded appearance of the 'rogues' denounced by him had for its object the rescue of some prisoners whom he had sent from Dumfries to Edinburgh under the escort of a detachment of his dragoons. A carefully planned ambush was laid by a number of armed men, amongst whom some English borderers were said to be. The spot chosen as most favourable for it was near Enterkin hill, 'where there is a very strait road and a deep precipice on both sides.' Taken at a disadvantage in this narrow pass, the soldiers of whom several were killed at the first discharge, had but slight chance of success against superior numbers. The accounts of the encounter differ from each other as regards several details ; but they leave no doubt about this one fact, at least, that the dragoons were worsted, and that it was with at most two of their prisoners only that they succeeded in reaching Edinburgh.

This daring act of aggression called forth fresh measures on the part of the Government. On the 1st of August, the Privy Council passed an Act redistributing the cavalry through the country, with a view to the more effectual suppression of ' all such rebellious courses for the future.' Claverhouse's troop of Guards, and that of his friend Lord Ross, together with two troops of dragoons, respec- tively commanded by Captain Inglis and Captain Cleland, were ordered for service in Ayrshire. In addition to this, Claverhouse was appointed, with Lieutenant-Colonel Buchan as his second, to command all the forces, ' foot, and horse, and dragoons, in the shires of Ayr and Clydesdale.' Further, to the effect that discovery might be made of the rebels in arms, and of such as had been present at field conventicles, the two officers were empowered and commissioned to call for and examine upon oath, all persons able to supply any information, and to use all legal diligence for that purpose.

In accordance with his new commission, Claverhouse again swept the south-western shires in every direction. If the actual capture of rebels be taken as the standard by which to estimate the result of his efforts, it appears to have been absolutely null. In spite of the promptitude of his movements, and in spite, too, of the care which he took to conceal them, it was impossible for him to secure secrecy. No sooner was his arrival known at any point than the news of his presence was spread through the surrounding country ; and when his search through the wild moorlands and over the pathless hills began, those whom he hoped to surprise were either in safe hiding or beyond the reach of his troopers. 'They have such intelligence,' he wrote to Queensberry on the 5th of August, 'that there is no surprising them ' ; and he added, with something of despondency in his tone, ' I fear we do nothing.' But, on the other hand, his success in temporarily clearing the district of conventiclers appears to have been rapid. Before the end of the same month he was able to delegate his duties to his subordinates, and to retire for a short time to Dudhope.

During his stay he had occasion to exercise, probably for the first time, his power as Constable of Dundee. The way in which he did so is set forth in the Register of the Privy Council :—'Edinburgh, 10th September 1684.—Whereas, it being represented to the Lords of his Majesty's Privy Council by Colonel Graham of Claverhouse, Constable of Dundee, that there are several prisoners in the Tolbooth of that burgh for petty or small thefts, or picking, which will be fitter to be punished arbitrarily than by death ; the said Lords do therefore give full power and commission to the said Colonel Graham of Claverhouse, Constable of Dundee, to restrict the punishment appointed by law, against such persons within his jurisdiction already made prisoners, or that shall hereafter be made prisoners upon account of the foresaid petty and small thefts, or picking, to an arbitrary punishment, such as whipping, or banishment, as he shall find cause.'

VI

THE KILLING TIME

THE last year of the reign of Charles II. was marked by a recrudescence of fanaticism on the part of the Covenanting extremists. It found expression in an 'apologetical declaration' drawn up by Renwick, and ordered to be affixed, as though it were a royal proclamation, 'upon a sufficient and competent number of the public market-crosses of the respective burghs, and of the patent doors of the respective kirks within this kingdom.' This document disowned the authority of Charles Stuart, and threatened to inflict the severest punishment, not only on those who were actively employed in enforcing the penal laws, 'such as bloody militia men, malicious troopers, soldiers and dragoons,' but also on the 'viperous and malicious bishops and curates,' and all such sort of counsellors and 'intelligencers.'

This 'declaration' was dated the 28th of October 1684, and was promulgated on the 8th of November. It appeared so outrageous even to some of the Covenanters themselves, that they denounced it as 'but a State invention, set on foot by the soldiers, to make that party odious and themselves necessary.' But before many days these sceptics were to be convinced 'of the reality of this declared war.' On the 20th of November news reached Edinburgh that, the night before, some of the desperate fanatics had broken in upon two of the King's Life Guards—Thomas Kennoway and Duncan Stewart—who were lying at Swyne Abbey, beyond Blackburn, in Linlithgowshire, and murdered them most barbarously. 'This,' adds Fountainhall, one of the contemporary chroniclers of the incident, 'was to execute what they had threatened in their declaration.'

This was not the only act of violence by which Renwick's proclamation was followed. Within the next month there

occurred two others, of which the scene lay within the district committed to the care of Claverhouse. The prompt and
successful measures which he took to punish the perpetrators
supply the elements of fact which partisan writers have dis-
torted and exaggerated into one of the most wanton atrocities
of the 'killing times'; and much may be learnt from an
examination of the whole episode in its successive phases.

It opens with the murder of the curate of Carsphairn on the night between the 11th and the 12th of
December. The victim was Mr Peter Peirson. The
worst of the unsubstantiated charges brought against him
by Wodrow, who, whilst professing to abhor and detest
the crime, is nevertheless at great pains to find extenuating
circumstances in the 'unwarrantable provocations this ill
man gave,' amount to this, that he was a surly, ill-natured
man, and horridly severe ; that he was very blustering and
bold, and used openly to provoke the poor people by
saying in public companies, 'He feared none of the Whigs,
nor anything else but rats and mice'; that he was openly
a favourer of popery, and not only defended the doctrine
of purgatory, but also declared openly that Papists were
much better subjects than Presbyterians ; that he was
a notorious informer and instigator of all the violent
measures resorted to in that part of the country ; and
that be kept a number of fire-arms loaded in his chamber
—a precautionary measure for which justification might be
found in the fact that the curate lived at the manse alone,
without so much as a servant with him.

Towards the end of the year 1684, a number of the
'wanderers' who were hiding in the neighbourhood 'entered
into a concert with an express proviso of doing no harm to
Mr Peirson's person, to meet together and essay to force
him to give a written declaration that he would forbear
instigating their enemies and other violent courses, and
deter him from them in time to come, still expressly declaring
they would do him no bodily harm.' In view of the sequel,
even as it is narrated by Wodrow himself, it would be super-
fluous to discuss the veracity of the whole statement as to
the innocent 'concert,' and still more so to inquire into

the sincerity of the alleged declaration. It may, however, be incidentally recalled that the murderers of Archbishop Sharp were asserted by Covenanting apologists to have come together for the harmless purpose of intimidating the obnoxious Carmichael, or as it was still more mildly expressed, of scaring him from his cruel courses, when chance threw the prelate in their way.

On the occasion, now under consideration, the circumstances that led to the tragic termination of the peaceful errand on which M'Michael, Padzen, Mitchell, Herron, Watson and some others were engaged are thus set forth: 'One night, having notice that Mr Peirson was at home, they came to the manse and sent those named above to desire Mr Peirson to speak with some friends who were to do him no harm. One account says, and it is not inconsistent with the other, that two of them who were sent, got in and delivered the commission, which put Mr Peirson in a rage, and, drawing a broadsword, and cocking a gun or pistol, he got betwixt them and the door; upon which they called, and M'Michael and Padzen came to the door and knocked. The other account makes no mention of this circumstance, but says when they knocked at the door, Mr Peirson opened it himself, and, with fury, came out upon them with arms; and James M'Michael, as he said, laying his account with present death if he had not done it, resolved, if he could, to be beforehand with him, and firing a pistol at him, shot him dead on the spot. The rest, at some distance, hearing a noise, came running up crying, "take no lives"; but it was too late.'

A few days after the murder of the curate, a body of 'Wanderers' committed a more open act of violence in the town of Kirkcudbright. According to Sir Robert Dalziel's official report to Queensberry, upon the Tuesday morning preceding the 18th of December, they invaded the town, to the number of a hundred and eight, broke open the prisons, carried away such prisoners as would go with them, and all the arms they could seize on, together with the town drum. It was then that Claverhouse set out in pursuit of the rioters. The accounts of his expedition are interesting in their variations from each other and from actual facts.

In the volume entitled 'A Cloud of Witnesses for the Royal Prerogatives of Jesus Christ,' there is a section specially devoted to an enumeration of those 'who were killed in the open fields, without trial, conviction, or any process of law, by the executioners of the Council's murdering edict.' On the authority of 'A Short Memorial of the Sufferings and Grievances of the Presbyterians in Scotland,' printed in the year 1690, it is there stated that Claverhouse coming to Galloway, in answer to the Viscount of Kenmure's letter, with a small party, surprised Robert Stewart, John Grier, Robert Ferguson, and James MacMichael, and instantly shot them dead at the water of Dee. It is added that their corpses having been buried, were, at his command, raised again.

The same incident is reported by De Foe, with the addition of certain details that enhance its atrocity. In his summary of the cold-blooded cruelties perpetrated by the most furious persecutor of the 'poor people,' he has the following entry: 'Four more men who were betray'd to him, being hid in a house at the water of Dee, and were at the time his men came praying together; he caused them to be dragged just to the door, and shot them dead as they came out, without any enquiry whether they were the persons that he came to apprehend; their being found praying to God was, it seems, sufficient testimony of their party and offence; after this, coming to the same place, at two or three days' distance, and understanding the people of the town had buried the bodies, he caused his men to dig them up again, and commanded that they should lye in the fields: the names of these four were John Grier, Rober Ferguson, Archibald Stewart, and Robert Stewart.'

It will be noticed that the name of Archibald Stewart figures in this list instead of that of James MacMichael. Whether accidental or intentional the substitution is of considerable importance, as the sequel will show.

Without any intention of palliating the conduct of Claverhouse, Wodrow helps to place it in a different light.

'Let me add,' he says, 'that December 18th, Claverhouse when ranging up and down Galloway, with a troop, came to the water of Dee; and at Auchinloy, came upon some of the people, who were lurking and hiding, unexpectedly, and surprised six of them together; for what I can find, they had no arms. According to the instructions lately given by the Council, he shot four of them upon the spot in a very few minutes, Robert Ferguson and James Mac-Michan from Nithsdale, and Robert Stewart and John Grier, Galloway men; afterwards their friends carried off their bodies to Dalry and buried them. Some accounts before me say that by orders from Claverhouse, a party came and uncovered their graves and coffins, and they continued so open four days till the party went off. And it appears certain, that James MacMichan's body, after it was buried, was taken up and hung up on a tree. This was strange barbarity and spite. The other two, Robert Smith in Glencairn parish, and Robert Hunter, Claverhouse carried with him to Kirkcudbright, and called an assize, and made a form of judging them, and caused execute them there. They would not permit these two to write anything, not so much as letters to their relations. There were two more in the company who escaped and happy it was for them it was so, for probably they would have gone the same way.'

Wodrow admits that 'it may be the rescue of some prisoners of Kirkcudbright by some of the wanderers a little before this, was the pretext for all this cruelty.' But he says no word from which it can be gathered that the party which broke open the Tolbooth of Kirkcudbright could reasonably be suspected of including some of the men who murdered Peirson. He gives no hint of his knowledge that it was whilst pursuing these rioters that Claverhouse came upon the Deeside fugitives; and it almost seems as though, by a slight change of name, he wished to conceal the fact that the James Macmichan, whose body was treated with such 'strange barbarity and spite,' was no other than the James Macmichael whom he himself names as the actual murderer of Peirson.

The information which he failed to supply may be got from

Fountainhall, who, in his 'Historical Notices,' under date of the 20th of December, announces the receipt of letters from Claverhouse, reporting that he had met with a party of the rebels, who had skulked, that he had followed them, killed five, and taken three prisoners, some of whom were the murderers of the minister of Carsphairn, and that he was to judge and execute the three prisoners by his justiciary powers.

Such is the origin and development of one of those 'atrocities' to which Claverhouse owes the opprobrious epithet of 'bloody.'

For an impartial judgment of the extent of Claverhouse's personal connection with some of the incidents of this particular period, it must be remembered that early in the year Colonel Douglas was appointed on special duty against the 'Western fanatics.' In addition to this, on the 27th of March, the judicial powers previously held by Claverhouse were also conferred on Douglas, as Justice in all the southern and western shires. The instructions given him by the Privy Council contained a special clause referring to the treatment of women that might be brought before him or any of the members of his Commission. Only such as had been active in a signal manner in treasonable courses were to be examined; and those if found guilty, were to be drowned.

It was in accordance with this provision that Margaret Maclachlan and Margaret Wilson were condemned to death. Whether the sentence was actually carried out, or whether the account of their drowning on the sands of the Solway Firth given by Wodrow and repeated by Macaulay be wholly apocryphal, as Napier maintained, is a question into which it is not necessary to enter, though the difficulty of believing that so circumstantial a narrative can be a mere Covenanting fiction may readily be admitted. But it is not unimportant to point out that Claverhouse was neither directly nor indirectly concerned either in the trial, the sentence, or the execution, and that, though still nominally a Privy Councillor when Douglas superseded him, he was absent from the meeting at which his rival was appointed

Justice, and at which the drowning of women was ordered.

From the command of his own regiment, Claverhouse had not been removed. In the discharge of the duties which this position laid on him, he was brought into immediate connection with another incident which is commonly adduced as illustrative of the atrocities committed during the 'killing time,' but of which the real nature, terrible at best, it cannot be denied, is materially affected by the truth or the falseness of the details which have found their way into some accounts of the event. Claverhouse's report of the occurrence is contained in the following despatch forwarded to Queensberry from Galston on the 3rd of May 1685.

'On Friday last, amongst the hills betwixt Douglas and the Ploughlands, we pursued two fellows a great way through the mosses, and in the end seized them. They had no arms about them, and denied they had any. But, being asked if they would take the abjuration, the eldest of the two, called John Brown, refused it. Nor would he swear not to rise in arms against the King, but said he knew no king. Upon which, and there being found bullets and match in his house, and treasonable papers, I caused shoot him dead; which he suffered very unconcernedly.

'The other, a young fellow and his nephew, called John Brownen offered to take the oath; but would not swear that he had not been at Newmills in arms, at rescuing of the prisoners. So I did not know what to do with him. I was convinced that he was guilty, but saw not how to proceed against him. Wherefore, after he had said his prayers, and carbines presented to shoot him, I offered to him that if he would make an ingenuous confession, and make a discovery that might be of any importance for the King's service, I should delay putting him to death, and plead for him. Upon which he confessed that he was at that attack at Newmills, and that he had come straight to this house of his uncle's, on Sunday morning.

'In the time he was making this confession, the soldiers found out a house in a hill, under ground, that could hold a dozen of men, and there were swords and pistols in it; and this fellow declared that they belonged to his uncle, and that he had lurked in that place ever since Bothwell, where he was in arms. He confessed that he had a halbert, and told who gave it him about a month ago, and we have the fellow prisoner. He gave an account of the names of the most part who were there. They were not above sixty, and they were all Galston and Newmills men, save a few out of Straven parish. He gave also an account of a conventicle kept by Renwick at the back of Cairntable, where there were thirteen score of men in arms, mustered and exercised, of which number he was with his halbert. He tells us of another conventicle, about three months ago, kept near Loudon hill; and gives account of the persons who were at both, and what children were baptized; particularly that at Cairntable, which was about the time that Lieu-tenants Murray and Creichton let them escape. He also gives account of those who gave any assistance to his uncle; and we have seized thereupon the goodman of the upmost Ploughlands; and another tenant, about a mile below that, is fled upon it.

'I doubt not, if we had time to stay, good use might be made of his confession. I have acquitted myself, when I have told your Grace the case. He has been a month or two with his halbert; and if your Grace thinks he deserves no mercy, justice will pass on him. For I, having no commission of Justiciary myself, have delivered him up to the Lieutenant-General, to be disposed of as he pleases.'

Such a report is not that of a man anxious to urge excuses for an action which he felt in his conscience to be unjustifiable. Nor can there be any doubt that, from his point of view, Claverhouse had done nothing but what a soldier's duty required of him. Immediately after the pro-clamation of Renwick's manifesto, and the subsequent murder of the two guardsmen at Swyne Abbey, it had been enacted that 'Any person who owns or will not disown the late treasonable declaration on oath, whether they have arms or not, be immediately put to death, this being always done in the presence of two witnesses, and the person or persons having commission to that effect.'

Such was the law; and the blind obedience to orders which Claverhouse looked upon as a part of his duty as a soldier, on which he prided himself, and which, as has been seen, he declared in so many words to be his one guiding principle, left him no option as to enforcing it in the case of John Brown. With respect to the nephew, on the other hand, the same spirit of strict discipline forbade him to inflict summary punishment, not because he thought him less guilty than the uncle, but because he had complied with the letter of the law. If further action were to be taken in the case, it would have to be by those who possessed that power of justiciary of which he had been deprived.

This John Brown who was executed in due form of martial law is the 'Christian Carrier' whom Wodrow accuses Claverhouse of having killed with his own hand. After representing Brown as a man of 'shining piety,' who 'was no way obnoxious to the Government, except for not hearing the Episcopal minister,' and after stating that he was apprehended whilst 'at his work, near his own house in Priestfield, casting peats,' the historian continues: 'Claverhouse was coming from Lesmahagow, with three troops of dragoons: whether he had got any information of John's piety and nonconformity, I cannot tell, but he caused bring him up to his own door, from the place where he was. I do not find they were at much trouble with interrogatories and questions; we see them now almost wearied of that leisurely way of doing business, neither do any of my informations bear that the abjuration oath was offered him. With some difficulty he was allowed to pray, which he did with the greatest liberty and melting, and withal, in such suitable and scriptural expressions, and in a peculiar judicious style, he having great measures of the gift, as well as the grace of prayer, that the soldiers were affected and astonished; yea, which is yet more singular, such convictions were left in their bosoms, that, as my informations bear, not one of them would shoot him, or obey Claverhouse's commands, so that he was forced to turn executioner himself, and in a fret shot him with his own hand, before his own door, his wife with a young infant standing by, and she very near the time of her delivery of another child.   When tears and entreaties could not prevail, and Claverhouse had shot him dead, I am credibly informed the widow said to him, "Well, sir, you must give an account of what you have done."   Claverhouse answered, "To men I can be answerable, and as for God, I'll take Him into mine own hand."   I am well informed that Claverhouse himself frequently acknowledged afterwards that John Brown's prayer left such impressions upon his spirit that he could never get altogether worn off, when he gave himself liberty to think of it.'

A comparison of the two accounts might suffice to establish their respective credibility.   But another test is available.   There is a third version of the death of John Brown.   It is given by Patrick Walker, a pedlar and Covenanting martyrologist, who implies that he himself got it from Brown's widow, 'sitting upon her husband's gravestone.'   Apart from minor discrepancies between his narrative and that of Wodrow, there are at least three important points with regard to which it directly confirms Claverhouse's report.   It not only asserts that the carrier, when brought to his house, was examined by his captor, but it also adds that though a man of a stammering speech, he yet answered distinctly and solidly.   In contradiction of the statement that 'with some difficulty he was allowed to pray,' it represents Claverhouse as saying to him, 'Go to your prayers, for you shall immediately die.'   Most important of all, however, it affirms distinctly and circumstantially that 'Claverhouse ordered six soldiers to shoot him,' and that 'the most part of the bullets came upon his head, which scattered his brains upon the ground.'

Within a week after the shooting of John Brown, there occurred another execution, the responsibility for which has been laid on Claverhouse by several of the writers who chronicle the sufferings of the Covenanters at this time   The first of them is Alexander Shields.   'The said Claverhouse,' he says, ' together with the Earl of Dumbarton and Lieutenant-General Douglas, caused Peter Gillies, John Bryce, Thomas Young (who was taken by the Laird of Lee), William Fiddisone, and John Buiening to be put to death upon a gibbet, without legal trial or sentence, suffering them neither to have a Bible nor to pray before they died.' De Foe, whilst deepening the atrocity of the deed, allows no one to share the guilt of it with Claverhouse. According to him, somebody had maliciously told Graham that five men who lay in 'several prisons,' to which they had been committed by 'other persecutors,' were 'of the Whigs that used the field meetings; upon which, without any oath made of the fact, or any examination of the men, without any trial or other sentence than his own command, his bloody soldiers fetched them all to Mauchline, a village where his headquarters were, and hanged them immediately, not suffering them to enter into any house at their coming, nor at the entreaty of the poor men would permit one to lend them a Bible, who it seems offered it, nor allow them a moment to pray to God.'

The case of two of these men, that of Peter Gillies and John Bryce has been cited by Macaulay as one of the instances of the crimes by which Claverhouse and men like him, goaded the peasantry of the Western Lowlands into madness. His account, based on that given by Wodrow, refutes the statement made by De Foe as to the absence of all legal formality. He admits that the two artisans were tried by a military tribunal consisting of fifteen men; and thus sets aside what both Shields and De Foe put forward as the crowning atrocity of the deed. But, on the other hand, by mentioning the execution amongst other alleged instances of Claverhouse's cruelty, he leaves the reader under the impression that it was he and his dragoons who acted as judge and jury. Now Wodrow distinctly states that, on being taken to Mauchline, Gillies and Bryce, ' with some others, were examined by Lieutenant-General Drummond,' and that ' an assize was called of fifteen of the soldiers,' with Drummond himself as ' Commissioner of Justiciary.'

Claverhouse's name does not once occur in Wodrow's detailed account of the incident, and evidence to connect him directly and personally with the trial or execution is consequently wanting.

The last instance drawn from 'the history of a single fortnight,' of that lamentable month of May 1685, is the summary execution of Andrew Hislop, in Eskdale Muir. There are two accounts of it. One of them is to be found in 'The Cloud of Witnesses.' The other is given by Wodrow. About Hislop himself, the latter tells us that he was but a youth, and lived with his mother, to whom one of the 'suffering people' had come for shelter, and in whose house he had died. For her charity towards the proscribed Covenanter, and for affording his body burial, the poor widow brought down upon herself the vengeance of the Laird of Westerhall, who though 'once a Covenanter, a great professor and zealot for the presbyterian establishment,' had become a violent persecutor of his former brethren, 'as all apostates generally are.' To signalise his loyalty, Westerhall pulled down the woman's cottage, carried off everything that was portable, and drove her with her children into the fields. Her eldest son Andrew, however, was reserved for a worse fate, as to the actual circumstances of which there are conflicting narratives. That contained in the book commonly known as 'The Cloud of Witnesses' states that Westerhall delivered him up to Claverhouse, 'and never rested until he got him shot by Claverhouse's troops.' Wodrow, though he was acquainted with this account, and actually refers to it, so far departs from it as to make Claverhouse the lad's captor. 'Claverhouse,' he says, 'falls upon Andrew Hislop in the fields, May 10th, and seizes him, without any design, as appeared, to murder him, bringing him prisoner with him to Eskdale, unto Westerhall that night.'

To the first account, which is that favoured by Macaulay, there is this objection, that Claverhouse had been deprived of his judicial power, and, for that very reason had refused to deal with John Brown's nephew, and delivered him up to the Lieutenant-General. Westerhall, on the other hand, is stated by Wodrow to have been 'one empowered by the Council'; and that is probably why the historian inverts the parts played by the two respectively. But, against accepting his account, there is the difficulty of understanding how Westerhall allowed Hislop to escape from his clutches in the first instance. Whichever may be the true statement of the case, the sequel is practically identical according to both versions. 'Claverhouse,' says Wodrow, 'in this instance was very backward, perhaps not wanting his own reflections upon John Brown's murder, and pressed the delay of the execution. But Westerhall urged till the other yielded, saying, the blood of this poor man be upon you, Westerhall, I am free of it.' Thereupon, it is stated, Claverhouse ordered a Highland gentleman, who, with his company, was temporarily under his orders, to provide the firing-party. But the Captain, continues the account, peremptorily refused, and drawing off his men to a distance, swore he would fight Claverhouse and his dragoons rather than act the part of executioner. Three troopers were then called out, and Hislop fell before their fire.

There are circumstances that make it difficult to accept this statement of the case. If Claverhouse was averse to the summary execution of Hislop, it may very safely be assumed, on the strength of what is known concerning his character, that nothing but his respect for superior authority and the blind obedience to it, which he repeatedly declared to be his guiding principle as a soldier, would have induced him to take any part in it. In that case, the whole responsibility would be removed from him, and laid upon Westerhall, whose orders he merely carried out. But this substitution is not possible. As Claverhouse cannot but have known, Westerhall was not in a position to act as judge in the case; and there would consequently have been no breach and no infringement of the strictest discipline in disregarding commands which he was not justified in giving.

Wodrow, as has been seen, states that Westerhall was 'one empowered by the Council.' The commission to which this refers had been granted on the 3rd of January 1684; and, it may be incidentally mentioned that the power which it gave him to judge desperate rebels, could not be exercised by him individually and alone, but in conjunction with two other colleagues. But what Wodrow either overlooked or ignored, is the fact that, on the 21st of April 1685, General Drummond was invested with the whole authority previously held conjointly by the commissioners; and that the royal warrant by which this supersession was effected, expressly declared that all former commissions granted either by the King or by the Privy Council for trying or punishing criminals, were void and extinct. It consequently follows that if Claverhouse acted as he is alleged to have done, he did not merely consent, sullenly or otherwise, to the carrying out of a cruel and iniquitous, but strictly legal sentence, he actually became an accomplice in a deliberate murder of which he did not approve and which he could have prevented by taking up the same position as the Highland gentleman is said to have assumed. Were this the case, the shooting of Hislop would be one of the most indefensible of the atrocities with which Claverhouse has been charged. And yet we do not find that those who were watching his conduct at the time with all the keenness of enmity, and who would gladly have availed themselves of such an opportunity for doing him an ill turn, took any notice of the occurrence.

Still more convincing is it, that the Covenanting writers who record the incident, whilst bitter enough in their denunciations of Claverhouse's inhumanity, are absolutely silent as to the lawlessness of his action. This difficulty has been met by the suggestion that there were probably other proceedings, of which the accounts omit to make mention; that Hislop was asked to take the oath, and, by refusing to do so, made himself amenable to the full penalty of the law. Such an assumption clears both Westerhall and Claverhouse of the actual guilt of murder. It does not free the latter from the charge of having acted with a weakness and a subserviency as unjustifiable in themselves as they seem foreign to his nature. Under the circumstances, the least that can be claimed for him is an open verdict. To convict him on such evidence as has been adduced, and to do so for the purpose of vindicating the veracity of writers who are not even in accord with each other would be palpably unjust.

Matthew Meiklewrath is another of the victims of this terrible time; and if the account of his death given by De Foe were as accurate as it is circumstantial, no term but that of murder could be applied to the outrage alleged to have been committed by Claverhouse. 'At Comonel, in the County of Carrick,' states the chronicler of his misdeeds, 'he saw a man run hastily across the street before his troop, and as he might suppose did it to escape from or avoid them, though, as the people of the place related it, the poor man had no apprehensions of them, but as he took all occasions for his bloody designs, he commanded his men to shoot this person, without so much as examining him, or asking who he was.' The refutation of this charge of wanton barbarity is to be found in the epitaph quoted in 'The Cloud of Witnesses' from a stone in the churchyard where Meiklewrath was interred :—

> 'In this parish of Colmonel,
> By bloody Claverhouse I fell,
> Who did command that I should die,
> For owning covenanting Presbytery.
> My blood a witness still doth stand,
> 'Gainst all defections in this land.'

The cases that have been cited do not exhaust the black list that might be drawn up from the accounts already referred to. They may suffice, however, to show, not indeed that Claverhouse performed the odious duties imposed upon him by his position otherwise than sternly and remorselessly, but, at least, that the most notorious of the instances which represent him as going far beyond even what the merciless laws required or authorised, as delighting in suffering and revelling in bloodshed, are demonstrably exaggerations, and that impartial investigation, whilst it may lead us to deplore the relentless severity with which he carried out the orders of the Government, does not justify us in holding him up to obloquy as a monster of cruelty.

VII

CHARLES II. died at the beginning of February 1685, and
was succeeded by his brother. As Duke of York James
had been Claverhouse's chief patron; as King, one of his
first actions was to express his disapproval of the conduct
to which his favourite had been urged by a 'high, proud
and peremptory humour.' This was the result of a quarrel
with Queensberry, of which the origin, trifling in itself,
went back to the beginning of the previous December.
At a meeting of the Privy Council, held on the 11th
of that month, there was read a complaint presented
by some soldiers whom Queensberry's brother, Colonel
James Douglas had turned out of his regiment, and who
alleged that their commanding officer 'had taken the
arrears of their pay, and clothed and shoed some of the
rest of the soldiers therewith.' The complainant's cause
was taken up by Claverhouse, on the ground that the
treatment to which they had been submitted would dis-
courage others from entering into his Majesty's service.
This the High Treasurer resented as reflecting on the
manner in which his brother had done his duty; and thus,
says Fountainhall, grew the difference between him and
Claverhouse.

Whatever may have been the intrinsic merits of the case,
and it is but fair to state that Douglas had otherwise shown
himself a zealous and capable officer, there can be no doubt
that Claverhouse had put himself in the wrong, by allowing
his temper to get the better of him. This he himself
admitted in a letter which he wrote to James, and in which
he endeavoured 'to excuse his warmth by saying he took
what was said as levelled at him.' But after reading this

account and comparing it with that which he also received, not from Queensberry, but from 'both the Chancellor and Lundy,' the Duke was obliged to express his regret 'that Claverhouse was so little master of himself the other day at Council,' and promised that when he came to Scotland he would let the offender know that his behaviour was not approved of.

James's accession prevented his leaving London at the time, as he had apparently intended to do. It was also the cause of Queensberry's being summoned to Court. It may be assumed that during his stay the quarrel with Claverhouse formed the subject of conversation between him and the King; but there is nothing to show that he solicited further satisfaction than had already been given him by the appointment of Douglas to the command of the forces in the western shires, in supersession of Colonel Graham. When he returned to Scotland at the end of March as Lord High Commissioner to the Scottish Parliament, he does not appear to have known that it was the King's intention to take further cognizance of the matter.

It was from Secretary Murray that he learnt Claverhouse's exclusion from the Privy Council, 'to show him and others that his Majesty would support his Minister, and not suffer any to do unfit or misbecoming things.' The letter conveying the information was written on the 5th of April. Four days later a new Commission was produced at the Board, from which none of the former Privy Councillors but Claverhouse was omitted. Amongst the better informed, there was no doubt that this was 'because of the discords between him and the High Treasurer and his brother,' as Fountainhall asserts. But the same authority states the 'pretence' to have been 'that having married into the Lord Dundonald's fanatic family, it was not safe to commit the King's secrets to him.'

While thus indicating his dissatisfaction with Claverhouse, James felt that the whole quarrel was too petty to justify him in punishing with lasting disgrace a faithful servant whose valuable help he had repeatedly acknowledged. He was at special pains to let him understand that if he tendered an apology to Queensberry he should be restored to place and favour. There is no direct evidence of submission on Claverhouse's part; but, that his better sense, or, to put it at its lowest, a saner appreciation of his own interest soon prevailed over his pride may be gathered from the fact that a royal letter, dated the 11th of May, reinstated him as Privy Councillor.

Within a fortnight of his reappointment he received further proof of the value set on his services. About this time news had arrived of Argyle's intended invasion of Scotland, and it would seem that Claverhouse had communicated some important information with regard to it, in a despatch to the Lord Commissioner. The document is not known to be extant; but its purport is indicated by the reply which it elicited from the Secret Committee of Council, and which was written on the 23rd of May. 'If there be any danger by horse,' he was told, 'it must be from the Border'; and he was authorised to propose what he judged expedient with a view to meeting the emergency, and instructed to inform the Earl of Dumbarton, who had just received his commission as Commander-in-Chief, of the measures which he intended to adopt. He was also to keep in touch with Fielding the deputy-governor of Carlisle. This clearly shows that the danger which he apprehended and had pointed out threatened the disaffected western counties.

The discretionary powers with which the letter of the Council invested Claverhouse implied the recognition, not very willing, it may be assumed, on the part of all the 'affectionate friends and servants' who signed it, and at the head of whom Queensberry figured as Commissioner, of his special fitness to cope with it. But the most striking and interesting passage in the document consists of a couple of lines, thrown in almost casually, and curtly announcing his promotion. 'The King has sent commissions to Colonel Douglas and you as Brigadiers, both of horse and foot. Douglas is prior in date.' When it is remembered in what relation Claverhouse had stood to Queensberry and his brother, but a short time before, the ungracious tone of this communication becomes highly suggestive. The suspicions which it arouses are amply confirmed by a full statement of the case, as it is set forth by Secretary Murray in a confidential letter to Queensberry. There could be no more striking proof of the feelings of ill-will and of envy which Claverhouse had to contend against, on the part of the Government, or of the intrigues that were resorted to by his opponents :—

'The King ordered two commissions to be drawn, for your brother and Claverhouse to be Brigadiers. We were ordered to see how such commissions had been here, and in Earl Middleton's office we found the extract of one granted to Lord Churchill, another to Colonel Worden, the one for horse, the other for foot. So Lord Melfort told me the King had ordered him to draw one for your brother for the foot, and Claverhouse for the horse. I told him that could not be ; for by that means Claverhouse would command your brother. To be short, we were very hot on the matter. He said he knew no reason why Colonel Douglas should have the precedency unless that he was your brother. I told him that was enough ; but that there was a greater, and that was, that he was an officer of more experience and conduct, and that was the King's design of appointing Brigadiers at this time. He said Claverhouse had served the King longer in Scotland. I told him that was yet wider from the purpose ; for there were in the army that had served many years longer than Claverhouse, and of higher quality ; and without disparagement to any, gallant in their personal courage. By this time I flung from him, and went straight to the King, and represented the case. He followed and came to us. But the King changed his mind, and ordered him to draw the commissions both for horse and foot, and your brother's two days date before the other ; by which his command is clear before the other. I saw the commissions signed this afternoon, and they are sent herewith by Lord Charles Murray. Now, I beseech your Grace, say nothing of this to any ; nay, not even to your brother. For Lord Melfort said to Sir Andrew Forrester, that he was sure there would

H

be a new storm on him. I could not, nor is it fit this should have been kept from you; but you will find it best for a while to know, or take little notice; for it gives him but ground of talking, and serves no other end.'

Even if Queensberry was as discreet as his correspondent advised him to be, there is no reason for supposing that Melfort considered himself bound to keep Claverhouse in ignorance of the stormy scene described by Murray. But although the newly-promoted Brigadier must have been well aware of the device by which his enemies had found means of coupling a slight with what was intended to be a mark of royal favour, he had the wisdom and the self-restraint to show no consciousness of it. A letter which he wrote to Queensberry on the 16th of June, bears testimony to his calm and self-respecting conduct, whilst, at the same time, it shows that the Lord Commissioner was as spitefully intent as ever on finding opportunities or excuses for annoying and humiliating him.

Documents for the reconstruction of the whole case are not available. All that can be ascertained is that, in carrying out the precautionary measures which his additional powers justified and which the emergency required, he had requisitioned the assistance of some of Queensberry's tenants. This had been construed into an offence, and made the subject of a report to the commander-in-chief who had no course open to him but that of intimating the Duke's displeasure to his subordinate. The reply, addressed to Queensberry himself was respectful but dignified. 'I am sorry,' he wrote, 'that anything I have done should have given your Grace occasion to be dissatisfied with me, and to make complaints against me to the Earl of Dumbarton. I am convinced your Grace is ill informed; for after you have read what I wrote to you two-days ago on that subject, I daresay I may refer myself to your own censure. That I had no design to make great search there anybody may judge. I came not from Ayr till after eleven in the forenoon, and went to Balagen, with forty heritors against night. The Sanquar is just in the road; and I used these men I met accidentally on the road better than ever I used any in these circumstances. And

I may safely say, that, as I shall answer to God, if they had been living on my ground, I could not have forborne drawing my sword and knocking them down.   However, I am glad I have received my Lord Dumbarton's orders anent your Grace's tenants, which I shall most punctually obey; though, I may say, they were safe as any in Scotland before.'

With this explanation, the matter appears to have been dismissed from Claverhouse's mind; and the remainder of his letter is taken up with remarks concerning certain dispositions intended by the other commanders who, like himself, were watching the progress of the threatened invasion.   His outspoken, but well-grounded criticism of them showed that the rebuke administered to him had not reduced him to a condition of cringing subserviency, and that the obedience which he was prepared to yield to those in authority above him did not include a readiness to bear responsibility for the result of measures which seemed to him ill-advised.

The extant correspondence between Claverhouse and Queensberry closes with a letter bearing date of the 3rd of July 1685.   It is a report as to the manner in which an order from the Secret Committee with regard to the disposal of the moveables of rebels for the maintenance of the royal forces had been carried out.   It is a straightforward and business-like statement, setting forth how the money already received had been laid out, and requesting instructions with respect to the sums still due.

Apart from the desire which every honourable man would feel, and with which Claverhouse may be credited, of placing himself above suspicion in all that concerned the management of the funds that came into his hands, he had special reason for exercising exceptional care in the matter in view of the humiliating treatment to which he had been subjected shortly before.   In the preceding month of March, Queensberry, as High Treasurer had given orders to the cashkeeper to charge Claverhouse on a bond he had given to the Exchequer, for the fines of delinquents in Galloway. Claverhouse had replied that his brother, the Sheriff-

depute, was gathering them in, and craved for delay,
whereupon he was allowed five or six days' grace.   He
objected that considering the distance, such a concession
was as unreasonable as giving no time at all.   To this the
Treasurer had retorted, 'Then you shall have none.'

Claverhouse had paid the money ; but he was not content
to remain under the imputation which Queensberry's action
towards him implied.   He had repeatedly applied for leave
to proceed to London, for the purpose of explaining his
conduct to the King, both in this transaction and in other
matters which had been made the grounds of complaints
against him, and which had led to his temporary disgrace.
He had been persistently refused, and it was not till the
end of the year that he had an opportunity of pleading his
cause before James.   Then, however, he did it to good
purpose.   According to Fountainhall, 'the King was so ill-
satisfied with what the Treasurer had exacted of Claverhouse, that he ordered the Treasurer to repay it.'

On the 24th of December 1685, Claverhouse returned
to Edinburgh in company with the Earl of Perth.   The
Chancellor had recently abjured Protestantism, and stood
in high favour with the King.   But if, as Halifax sar-
castically remarked, his faith saved him at Court, it made
him impossible in Scotland.   Within a few weeks of his
arrival, on Sunday, the 31st of January, there was a popular
demonstration against the avowed and public meetings
for the celebration of Mass and other acts of 'Papish
worship.'   The disorderly crowd, in which the apprentices
of Edinburgh figured conspicuously, fell upon one of the
priests, and compelled him, under threats of death, to
renounce popery, and, on bended knees, to take the test
oath.   Others, as they came from church, were roughly
treated and had mud thrown at them.

One of the victims of this popular violence was the Chancellor's wife.   The Earl was so incensed at the outrage that
he caused some of the boys to be apprehended ; and, next
day, by order of the Council, one of them was taken to be
whipped through the Canongate.   But whilst the sentence
was being carried out, the apprentices again mustered in large

numbers, assaulted the executioner, and rescued their companion. Encouraged by their success, they became so riotous that the soldiers were called out. The crowd was fired upon, and three persons were killed. Next day further punishment was inflicted on the rioters. A woman and two men were flogged through the city; but the authorities had become so apprehensive of violence that the streets were lined with 'two thick ranks and defiles of musketeers and pikemen.'

Even the military could not be depended upon. A grenadier was remitted to a court-martial for saying he would not fight in the quarrel against the Protestants; and a drummer having been denounced by some Catholics for drawing his sword and declaring that he could find it in his heart to run it through them was summarily shot. Later, a fencing-master was condemned to death and hanged for publicly giving expression to his approval of the tumult. Another man who was brought before the magistrates on a charge of speaking against the Papists, would perhaps have shared the same fate, had it not been proved on his behalf, that he was sometimes mad.

The protest of the street was taken up by the pulpit. A fortnight later, 'Mr Canaires, lately Popish,' but now minister at Selkirk, preached a violent sermon in the High Church of Edinburgh. In the course of it he gave utterance to the opinion 'that no man, without renouncing his sense and reason,' could embrace such doctrines as those of the Pope's infallibility or of transubstantiation. At the next meeting of the Council, the Chancellor moved that notice should be taken of this seditious language. Fountainhall records that 'Claverhouse backed the Chancellor in this. But, there being a deep silence in all the rest of the Councillors, it was passed over at this time.'

With this incident, which the unquestioned sincerity of his own religious belief makes it impossible to regard in any light but that of a protest against the insult offered to his sovereign, Claverhouse disappears for a time from the scene. There is no record of personal action on his part for a space of nearly three years. The only two events

that have to be chronicled are his promotion, in 1686, to
the rank of Major-General, still in subordination to his
rival Douglas, and his appointment, in March 1688, to be
Provost of Dundee, a dignity which, in conjunction with
his Constable's jurisdiction, made him absolute there.

Early in the month of September 1688, a royal messenger
arrived in Edinburgh, bearing a letter in which James
informed the Secret Committee of the Privy Council of the
Prince of Orange's designs on England. The news was
wholly unexpected. So incredible did it at first seem, that
suspicions of a device for raising money were aroused by
it. The precautionary measures which the announcement
made it incumbent on the Government to take for the
security of the country, were nevertheless adopted without
delay. On the 18th, a proclamation was issued, calling out
the militia regiments and requiring all fencible men to hold
themselves in readiness for active service as soon as they
should see the light of the beacons that were to be kindled
the moment a hostile fleet was sighted from the coast.

These preparations were nullified by a second despatch
from London, which ordered all the regular troops to
proceed at once to England, where they were to be under
the orders of the Earl of Feversham, the commander-
in-chief of the King's forces. This new plan of action,
suggested by James Stewart of Goodtrees, a notorious
plotter who had actually been condemned to death for his
connection with Argyle's rebellion, and whose antecedents
were not such as to justify the King's confidence in him,
was received with consternation in Edinburgh. The
Council and Secret Committee, relying on the loyalty of
the army, felt satisfied of their power to keep the nation in
due respect; but they were fully alive to the danger which
would arise if the country were denuded of troops. They
accordingly sent a remonstrance to the King, at the same
time that they submitted a feasible and efficient scheme of
defence of their own. Its main features consisted in the
retention of the regular forces in their several garrisons, for
the maintenance of internal order, and in the protection of
the Border by means of an army of thirteen thousand men,

to be formed by a combination of the militia with the Highland clans.

This judicious advice was summarily rejected; and a further command was sent to the Council to carry out the former instructions. According to Balcarres, the order was positive and short, advised by Mr James Stewart at a supper, written upon the back of a plate, and immediately dispatched by an express. In the memoirs which the same writer addressed and presented to James in his exile, the sequel is thus narrated : 'With a sorrowful heart to all your servants, your orders were obeyed, and about the beginning of October they began their march, three thousand effective young men, vigorous, well-disciplined and clothed, and to a man hearty in your cause, and willing out of principle as well as duty, to hazard their lives for the support of the Government, as then established, both in Church and State.'

Of the army that marched into England, Claverhouse led the cavalry, which consisted of his own regiment of six troops, of Livingstone's troop of royal Horse Guards, and of Dunmore's regiment of dragoons. The infantry was under the orders of Douglas, who, in virtue of his rank as Lieutenant-General, was also entrusted with the supreme command of the whole force. The arrangements for the march appear to have been as inadequate as the order for it had been ill-advised. Writing to Queensberry on the 7th of October, Douglas reported that he had reached Moffat the evening before, with considerable difficulty, owing to the bad state of the roads. He was unprovided with ammunition, and all he knew concerning his present business was, that horses for his baggage were to be furnished him in England, during forty days, and that it was the King's wish that he should march to Preston and remain there till further orders.

At Aleson Bank, which he reached three days later, further cause for worry and annoyance awaited him. Conflicting instructions from the King and from Dumbarton left him in doubt whether he was to take the east or the west road to London. In any case, Claverhouse was to proceed to York with the cavalry; and Douglas's comment on this was that he had never seen such a course adopted before, to send away all the horse, and leave two regiments of foot open to the insults of foreigners, who were expected to land horse and dragoons.

Fully a month had elapsed since the departure of Douglas and Claverhouse from Scotland before they reached London. After a few days' halt they started for Salisbury, where James had assembled an army of twenty-four thousand men, to oppose the Prince of Orange, who had landed at Torbay, on the 5th of November, and was advancing towards the capital. It was whilst on his march to join his sovereign that Claverhouse received a further and final token of royal favour by being created Viscount Dundee. He had left London on the 10th, and the patent of his peerage bore the date of the 12th of November 1688.

Before setting out for the camp at Salisbury, James had summoned his principal officers to him—Churchill, lately promoted Lieutenant-General, Grafton, colonel of the First Guards, Kirke and Trelawny, colonels of the Tangier regiments—and had received from them assurances of fidelity. Before the end of the month they had all deserted to William. Amongst the officers of the Scottish contingent, there was one also whose loyalty was unequal to the strain which circumstances put upon it. This was Lieutenant-General Douglas. When he went to England with the army, he was ignorant of the treasonable designs of some of his English brother officers; but he had not conversed long with Churchill, Kirke, and the others before he grew 'one of the hottest of the party.'

Balcarres, who brings the charge against him, asserts, on the authority of Dundee himself, that he proposed to his subordinate to betray the royal cause, and to take his regiment over with him. Before broaching the subject, however, he took the precaution of exacting an oath of secrecy. Though bound in honour to conceal his chief's disloyal overtures, Dundee may be supposed to have imposed conditions which Douglas thought it prudent to accept, and in accordance with which he maintained a show of allegiance for some time longer.

The Earl of Dumbarton was amongst the faithful few.
In his sturdy loyalty he offered, with his single regiment
of Scottish infantry to make a stand against the invading
forces of William.   A more practical suggestion was made
by Dundee.   With a generous confidence, says Dalrymple
in his " Memoirs," he advised his Majesty either to fight the
Prince, or to go to him in person and demand his business
in England.   But James chose to adopt a more spiritless
course, and retired from Salisbury.   According to the
account given by Creichton, who was serving at the time
in Dunmore's regiment of dragoons, Dundee was ordered
to bring up the Scottish horse to Reading, where he joined
Dumbarton with his forces, and remained for nine or ten
days.   'They were in all about ten thousand strong.
General Douglas, with his regiment of Foot Guards,
passing by Reading, lay at Maidenhead, from whence
one of his battalions revolted to the Prince, under the
conduct of a corporal whose name was Kemp.   However,
Douglas assured the King that this defection happened
against his will; and yet when the officers were ready to
fire upon the deserters, his compassion was such that he
would not permit them.'   After this, continues the same
narrator, the Earl of Dumbarton and Dundee, with all the
officers who adhered to the King, were ordered to meet his
Majesty at Uxbridge, where he intended to fight the Prince.
   When the forces had assembled at the place appointed,
each party sent an officer to the Earl of Feversham,
to receive his commands.   Creichton says that it was
he who attended on the part of Dundee, and that he
was ordered with the rest to wait till the King came
to dinner, his Majesty being expected within half-an-hour.
But matters took an unexpected turn.   The Earl, to his
great surprise, received a letter from the King, signifying
that his Majesty had gone off, and had no further service
for the army.   When Creichton returned with this news,
neither Dundee, nor Linlithgow, nor Dunmore could forbear bursting into tears.   It is further stated that Dundee,
acting upon a suggestion of which Creichton claims the
credit, had resolved to make his way back to Scotland,

when the townspeople, anxious to rid themselves as soon
as possible of the military, raised the report that the Prince
of Orange was approaching.   After preparation to receive
him had been hastily made, Creichton was again dispatched
by Dundee, to discover whether the alarm were true.   The
orderly was met on the way by a messenger whom William
had entrusted with a letter, of which the contents, quoted
from memory, are said to have been as follows :—

'MY LORD DUNDEE,—I understand you are now at
Watford, and that you keep your men together.   I desire
you will stay there till further orders, and upon my honour,
none in my army shall touch you.

'W. H. PRINCE OF ORANGE.'

From this point, there is some doubt as to Dundee's
movements.   He may, very probably, have gone on to
London ; and there is evidence of his having been there
shortly after the King's flight.   He was one of those who
attended a meeting of the Scottish Privy Councillors,
which had been hastily summoned by Balcarres to consider the situation, but which effected nothing beyond
affording Hamilton an opportunity of displaying his
'usual vehemency.'   If an account quoted by Napier
from 'Carte's Memorandum Book' is to be credited,
Dundee must, shortly after this, when the news of
James's arrest at Faversham reached the capital, have
gone to meet his luckless master at Rochester, and there
advised him to summon his disbanded army together again,
undertaking to raise ten thousand men himself, and to
march through all England with the royal standard at
their head.

There is better evidence of a final interview with James
after his return to London.   Besides Dundee himself,
Colin Earl of Balcarres was also present at it.   The Earl
had come for the purpose of making a last attempt to
move the King to active resistance, promising that if he
would but give the word, an army of twenty thousand
men would be ready to receive his orders.   The King,
however, had rejected the proposal ; and, as it was a fine

morning, expressed a wish to take a walk. Balcarres and Dundee accompanied him, 'When he was in the Mall, he stopped and looked at them, and asked how they could be with him, when all the world had forsaken him, and gone to the Prince of Orange. Colin said, their fidelity to so good a master would ever be the same, they had nothing to do with the Prince of Orange. Lord Dundee made the strongest professions of duty. "Will you two, as gentlemen, say you have still attachment to me?" "Sir, we do." "Will you give me your hands upon it, as men of honour?" They did so. "Well, I see you are the men I always took you to be; you shall know all my intentions. I can no longer remain here but as a cypher, or be a prisoner to the Prince of Orange, and you know there is but a small distance between the prisons and the graves of Kings. Therefore, I go to France immediately; when there, you shall have my instructions. You, Lord Balcarres, shall have a commission to manage my civil affairs, and you, Lord Dundee, to command my troops in Scotland."'

After the departure of James, both the noblemen remained in London for a time. It is stated by Dalrymple that both of them were asked by William to enter his service. 'Dundee,' he says, 'refused without ceremony. Balcarres confessed the trust which had been put in him, and asked the King if, after that, he could enter the service of another. William generously answered, 'I cannot say that you can;' but added, 'Take care that you fall not within the law, for otherwise I shall be forced, against my will, to let the law overtake you.'

Bishop Burnet puts a different complexion on the matter as regards Dundee; and it is his account that has led Macaulay to accuse the latter of having been less ingenuous than his friend Balcarres. The Bishop distinctly states that he himself had been employed by Dundee to carry messages from him to the King, to know what security he might expect, if he should go and live in Scotland without owning his government. 'The King said, if he would live peaceably and at home, he would protect him:

to this he answered that, unless he was forced to it, he would live quietly.'

It is not easy to believe that this is an absolutely accurate account of what actually took place. But the result, which scarcely amounts to a promise on the part of Dundee, as Macaulay interprets it, but rather appears in the light of a compromise on either side, is probably not far removed from the truth. It did not place Dundee in a special and exceptional position; it only put him on the same footing as all who were included in the general amnesty, not more generously than wisely, granted by William to the former adherents of the dethroned King. Of a personal interview between Dundee and William, there is no actual evidence.

By the beginning of 1689 there was no reason for further stay in England; and Dundee turned northwards again with Balcarres, and with the remnant of the cavalry at the head of which he had ridden to London in the autumn— a few troopers who had kept by their old chief even after their regiment was disbanded.

VIII

BEFORE THE STRUGGLE

WHEN Dundee reached Edinburgh, in the last days of February, the disturbances that had broken out shortly before had been quelled, owing mainly to the judicious and vigorous measures taken by the College of Justice; and to all outward appearance, at least, the capital was in a state of great tranquillity. But the excitement, though less demonstrative than it had been in the earlier weeks of the year, was still intense, and increased with the approach of the date fixed for the meeting of the Convention of the Estates, which was to determine whether England and Scotland were to be ruled by one sovereign, or whether there was to be a renewal between them of the hostilities of former centuries.

The Duke of Hamilton, the most influential of the Scottish noblemen who had offered their services to William, was making his arrangements in view of the coming crisis. He had brought in several companies of foot, which he billeted in the town. There seemed to be good reason to believe that before long he would be able to quarter them in the Castle. The command of the old fortress had been entrusted by James to the Duke of Gordon, 'a man weak and wavering in courage, but bound by shame and religion.' He had committed the almost inconceivable error of failing to provision the Castle, when he determined to hold it, and whilst the opportunity of procuring necessaries from the townspeople was still open to him. He had learnt that all the castles and forts in England had been given up, some of them, it was reported, by order of the exiled King himself; and no communication from any of his own party had brought

him encouragement to further resistance. When, on the
faith of a letter from William, he was offered indemnity
and full assurance of protection, he agreed to what, under
the circumstances, seemed to him to be an honourable
capitulation. He was in the very act of evacuating the
Castle, his furniture was actually being removed from it,
when Dundee and Balcarres came to him. By representing to him the service which he might still render
to the royal cause, and by appealing to his honour,
they succeeded in persuading him to hold out until the
Convention had given indications of its designs.

When the Estates met, on the 14th of March, Hamilton
secured a first victory for his party by getting himself
appointed President. At his suggestion, negotiations were
again opened with Gordon, by the intermediary of the
Earls of Lothian and Tweeddale. They were so far
successful that the wavering Governor promised to
surrender on the following day. But, when the time
came, he again evaded his engagement by insisting upon
terms which he knew could not be accorded him. It was
Dundee who had again worked the change. He had gone
to the Castle and assured Gordon that the King's friends
had resolved to desert the Edinburgh Convention, and
to summon another at Stirling, in virtue of the powers
given to the Archbishop of St Andrews, Balcarres, and
himself by a royal warrant received from Ireland. It is
asserted by Dalrymple that 'Balcarres, but still more
Dundee,' then urged the Governor to fire upon the city,
in order to dissolve the Convention. From the account
given by Balcarres, however, it would appear that this
advice was given by the King's 'friends' immediately after
Dundee had ridden off with his fifty troopers. For
failing to keep his engagement with the Convention,
Gordon was declared a traitor. As the heralds made
their proclamation in due form, under the very walls of
his fortress he spiritedly retorted that they ought in decency
to have doffed the King's livery before they proscribed
the King's governor.

It was true that, as Dundee had told Gordon, the

adherents of James had determined to desert the Convention. Their resolution was the result of an incident that had taken place at a recent sitting of that Assembly. Two letters had been received, one from the new King William, the other from the late King James. The former was read and 'answered in strains of gratitude and respect.' The latter met with a different reception. The members of the Orange party were at first unwilling that its contents should be made known. They urged that the nation would be in a miserable condition if the despatch should prove to be an order for the dissolution of the Convention. Many of their opponents admitted this. But they were confident that James had written 'in terms suitable to the bad situation of his affairs in England,' and had given such full satisfaction in matters of religion and liberty as would induce even most of those who had declared against him to return to their duty; and they consequently pressed that the message should be heard. It was not, however, until a unanimous vote had declared the Convention to be a legal and free meeting, and, as such, not to be dissolved by any order the letter might contain, that permission was granted. To the consternation of the Jacobites, and the joy of their enemies, it was found that the despatch, in which the hand and style of the obnoxious Melfort were recognised, 'was written in the terms of a conqueror and a priest, threatening the Convention with punishment in this world and damnation in the next.' There could no longer be any doubt as to what the result of the Convention would be.

The futility of making any further attempt to influence the Estates in favour of James was not the only reason that made Dundee desire to leave Edinburgh. He had received information that a number of his old enemies, the Covenanters, had formed a plot to assassinate him and Sir George Mackenzie. There can be no doubt that George Hamilton of Barns had brought up four hundred armed citizens from Glasgow, and had lodged them about the Parliament House; but it is alleged that the object of this measure was merely to prevent Dundee himself from carrying out a design which he had formed of seizing certain members of the Convention. At the next meeting of the Estates he made known what he had learnt, offered to point out the very house in which his intending murderers were concealed, and demanded that they should be brought to justice. A majority of the House refused to take cognisance of what was slightingly described as a private matter, until affairs of greater moment had been dealt with ; and Hamilton, who saw a welcome chance of getting rid of a troublesome adversary, cast sneering reflections upon the courage that could be alarmed by imaginary dangers.

This was on the eve of the day fixed upon by the Jacobite members for their departure from Edinburgh. In the meantime, however, the Marquis of Athole had pleaded for a further delay, and this had been agreed to at a meeting from which Dundee happened to be absent. When informed of the new arrangement, he refused to be bound by it. In vain Balcarres urged that his departure would give the alarm, and frustrate their designs. He replied that he had promised to meet a number of his friends outside the city, and that he did not wish to disappoint them. It was then that, going forth, he gathered his fifty troopers about him and galloped through the streets of Edinburgh. To a friend who called out to inquire where he was going, he is reported to have cried back, as he waved his hat, 'Wherever the spirit of Montrose shall direct me.'

Dundee's road to Stirling skirted the base of the Castle rock. As he approached he was recognised by the Duke of Gordon, who was 'in a manner blocked up by the western rabble,' and who signalled that he desired to speak with him. Equipped as he was, he performed the almost incredible feat of scrambling up the precipitous crag, as far as a postern gate, at which he held conference with the Governor. In the course of the conversation he urged the Duke to delegate the command of the stronghold to his subordinate Winrhame, an experienced and trustworthy soldier, and to retire into the Highlands for the purpose of raising his clansmen in support of King James. But Gordon's timidity suggested a ready and plausible excuse. A soldier, he said, could not in honour quit the post that had been assigned to him.

Whilst the two noblemen were conferring together under such unusual circumstances, they were noticed from the city. The troopers who were waiting below for their adventurous leader were magnified into a great body of horse, and it was assumed that Dundee's motive for braving the danger of such a climb, and defying the outlawry under which the Governor had been placed by the Convention, was to concert an attack in which he would be supported by the fire of the Castle batteries. The rumour spread and reached the ears of Hamilton. In all probability he knew it to be unfounded; but he also saw how he could avail himself of it to serve his own ends, and he did not neglect the opportunity which chance offered him. The Convention was sitting. With assumed indignation he exclaimed that it was high time they should look to themselves, since their enemies had the audacity to assemble in force, with hostile intent. Pretending to believe that there was danger within as well as without, he commanded the doors to be shut and the keys to be laid on the table before him, so that the traitors in their midst should be held in confinement until all danger from them was over. Then, by his orders, the drums were beat and the trumpets sounded through the city. At the signal, the armed men who had been brought in from the west, and hitherto kept concealed in garrets and cellars, swarmed out into the streets, where their fierce and sullen looks further increased the alarm of the townspeople, who gathered in great crowds about the Parliament House.

When the tumult and confusion had lasted for some hours, and long after the unconscious cause of it had resumed his ride, Hamilton, judging that the proper pitch had been reached, caused the doors to be thrown open again. As the members came out into the square, the Whigs 'were received with the acclamations, and those of the opposite party, with the threats and curses of a prepared populace.' The President had attained the object he had in view. As Dalrymple reports, 'terrified by the prospect of future alarms, many of the adherents of James quitted the Convention and retired to the country; more of them changed sides; only a very few of the most resolute continued their attendance.' The Whigs were left to themselves to settle the government of the country.

Whilst the Convention was still sitting with doors closed to prevent the egress of the Jacobite members, information was brought by Lord Montgomery, that Dundee had been seen going towards Queensferry after his defiant conference with the outlawed Duke of Gordon. Thereupon Major Buntin with a troop of horse was dispatched in pursuit. At the same time it was ordered that an express should be sent with a letter signed by the President, calling upon the deserter to return to the meeting by the following Friday. Whether it be true that the Major 'never came within sight' of the fugitive, or that he was scared by a threat of being sent back to his masters 'in a pair of blankets,' the result of his mission was the same.

The messenger may have found the means of delivering his letter at Linlithgow, where the Viscount made his first halt. It was possibly he who brought back the information which, on the next day, the 19th of March, caused the Convention to issue an order for the heritors and militia of Edinburgh and Linlithgow to assemble and 'dislodge' Lord Dundee. To give legal justification to these proceedings, an official proclamation was made by herald, charging both Dundee and Livingstone who accompanied him, to return to the Convention, within twenty-four hours, under pain of treason. Next day, a further report was received in Edinburgh, in consequence of which the Magistrates of Stirling were called upon to take suitable measures for seizing on the Viscount, who was understood to be in their neighbourhood. He had, in reality, ridden straight through to Dunblane, where he had an interview with Drummond of Balhaldy, who, as Lochiel's son-in-law, was doubtless able to give him useful information as to the condition of the Highlands, and where he also wrote to the Duke of

Hamilton, as President of the Convention, a letter which has not been preserved, and which may never have reached its destination. About the end of that eventful week, he reached his own home, at Dudhope. But, even here, he was not out of reach of heralds and their proclamations. On the 27th of March it was duly notified to him, with official blast of trumpet, that he was to lay down his arms, under penalty of being dealt with as a rebel to the State. His reply was almost suggested by the terms of the herald's summons. Dundee had no thought of accepting the new Government, and had never made a secret of his opposition to it. That he was fully prepared to take the field, if he saw a favourable opportunity of doing so, may be looked upon as the natural and necessary sequel to his acceptance of the trust verbally committed to him at his last meeting with James. But, so far, he had done nothing that justified the charge of having taken up arms. From that point of view, he had no difficulty in giving an explanation and a defence of his conduct. He did so in the following letter :—

DUDHOPE, *March* 27, 1689.

'MAY IT PLEASE YOUR GRACE,—The coming of an herald and trumpeter, to summon a man to lay down arms that is living in peace at home seems to me a very extraordinary thing, and, I suppose, will do so to all that hears of it. While I attended the Convention at Edinburgh, I complained often of many people being in arms without authority, which was notoriously known to be true; even the wild hillmen; and no summons to lay down arms under the pain of treason being given them, I thought it unsafe for me to remain longer among them. And because a few of my friends did me the favour to convey me out of the reach of these murderers, and that my Lord Livingstone and several other officers took occasion to come away at the same time, this must be called being in arms. We did not exceed the number allowed by the Meeting of Estates. My Lord Livingstone and I might have had each of us ten; and four or five officers that were in company might have had a certain number allowed them;

which being, it will be found we exceeded not.   I am sure
it is far short of the number my Lord Lorne was seen to
march with.   And though I had gone away with some
more than ordinary, who can blame me, when designs of
murdering me was made appear?   Besides, it is known
to everybody that, before we came within sixteen miles
of this, my Lord Livingstone went off to his brother my
Lord Strathmore's house; and most of the officers, and
several of the company, went to their respective homes or
relations.   And, if any of them did me the favour to come
along with me, must that be called being in arms.   Sure,
when your Grace represents this to the Meeting of the
States, they will discharge such a groundless pursuit, and
think my appearance before them unnecessary.   Besides,
though it were necessary for me to go and attend the
Meeting, I cannot come with freedom and safety; because
I am informed there are men of war, and foreign troops
in the passage; and, till I know what they are, and what
are their orders, the Meeting cannot blame me for not
coming.   Then, my Lord, seeing the summons has proceeded on a groundless story, I hope the Meeting of
States will think it unreasonable I should leave my wife
in the condition she is in.   If there be anybody that
notwithstanding of all that is said, think I ought to
appear, I beg the favour of a delay till my wife is brought
to bed; and, in the meantime, I will either give security,
or parole, not to disturb the peace.   Seeing this pursuit
is so groundless, and so reasonable things offered, and the
Meeting composed of prudent men and men of honour,
and your Grace presiding in it, I have no reason to fear
further trouble.—I am, may it please your Grace, your
most humble servant,   DUNDEE.'

'I beg your Grace will cause read this to the Meeting
because it is all the defence I have made.   I sent another
to your Grace from Dunblane, with the reasons of my
leaving Edinburgh.   I know not if it be come to your
hands.'

It is hardly probable that Dundee seriously expected

Hamilton and the Convention to be influenced in the course they were bent on adopting by a letter which, as regarded the past, contained little or nothing but what they had heard already, and which in respect to the future, bound the writer for a very limited period, in consideration of purely private and domestic, and not of political circumstances, except, perhaps, the circumstance that the instructions without which he was not to venture on any act of open hostility had not yet come from Ireland.

He cannot have been greatly surprised to learn that on the 30th of March he had formerly been declared a traitor.

Within less than a fortnight there occurred an incident which supplied Hamilton not only with a justification of the action he had taken, but also with a reason for adopting further measures against Dundee. The Viscount's commissions as Lieutenant-General and Commander-in-Chief in Scotland had been dispatched from Ireland. They were accompanied with letters from Melfort to both Dundee and Balcarres. To the former he wrote, ' You will ask, no doubt, how we shall be able to pay our armies : but can you ask such a question while our enemies, the rebels, have estates to be forfeited ? We will begin with the great, and end with the small ones.' The same sentiments were expressed in even stronger terms in his letter to the latter. ' The estates of the rebels will recompense us. You know there were several Lords whom we marked out, when you and I were together, who deserved no better fates ; these will serve as examples to others.' According to Balcarres, he added the senseless threat, 'when we get the power we will make these men hewers of wood and drawers of water.' Whether by the folly or the knavery of the bearer of them, these compromising documents fell into the hands of Hamilton. He communicated them to the Convention. When they had been read, he rose and cried out in an impetuous voice, 'You hear, you hear, my Lords and Gentlemen, our sentence pronounced. We must take our choice, to die, or to defend ourselves.'

The President had not waited for the decision of the Assembly. In virtue of the power given him at an earlier meeting, to imprison whomsoever he suspected to be acting against the common interest, he had sent a hundred men of the Earl of Leven's regiment into Fifeshire, and a like number into Forfarshire, to apprehend the two noblemen. Balcarres had already been brought back to Edinburgh and cast into prison. The knowledge that Dundee still had a number of his old troopers with him, did not help to stimulate the zeal of those to whom the duty of effecting his capture had been committed. Moreover, there lay between him and them two rivers, which necessitated a circuitous march. There had, consequently, been ample time for him to be informed of their approach ; and when they reach Dudhope, they learnt that their errand would be fruitless. Taking what was destined to be a last farewell of his wife and of his infant son, he retired towards the north.

But his retreat was not a flight. One of those who sallied forth with him, has described in scholarly Latin hexameters, how the gallant Graham mounted on his charger, brilliant in scarlet, in the face of the town, drew out in long line his band of brave youths, all mounted and in bright armour ; how, on the very top of the Law of Dundee, he unfurled the royal banner for the Northern war ; and how he triumphantly led the little troop of those who dared stand for the King in his misfortunes, over the lofty ridges of the Seidlaws, by Balmuir and Tealing, to his wife's jointure-house, in Glen Ogilvy. There he remained three days ; and Sir Thomas Livingstone, with his hundred men, marched after him, in the hope of being able to take him by surprise. But, 'though very well and secretly led on,' he was again too late. He returned to Dundee, whence he sent information of 'his mislucked design' to Mackay, whom William had appointed to the supreme command of the troops sent to Scotland, and where he was told to await the arrival of the General himself.

In the meantime, Dundee, who, at his interview with Lochiel's son-in-law, had been assured that as soon as he could get a body of troops together, the clans 'would risk their lives and fortunes under his command, and in King James's service,' was riding through the Highlands in the hope of enlisting recruits for the Stuart cause. From Dudhope, he had proceeded due north, through Glen Ogilvy, to the 'bare town' of Kirriemuir. Then crossing the Esk at the North Water Bridge, climbing the rugged heights of the Cairn-o'-Mount, and fording the Dee, he reached Kincardine O'Neil. By the 21st of April he was north of the Don, at Keith, where he made a brief halt, utilised for the purpose of attempting negotiations with Lord Murray. His next halting-place was Elgin, on the other side of the Spey, where the hospitality accorded him brought down the anger of the Convention on Provost Stewart and two of his bailies. Forres was the term of the rapid dash to the north, and there the little band again rested for a brief space.

During his progress through the Highland provinces, Dundee had not omitted the precaution of keeping up communication with the south; and he had received from his wife important information in accordance with which he at once devised a scheme of action. General Mackay was now in Scotland. On reaching Edinburgh he had received orders to march the forces which he had brought with him, and which consisted of three or four regiments of foot, and one of horse, besides Sir Thomas Livingstone's dragoons, against Lord Dundee. Leaving Sir John Lanier to carry on the siege of the Castle, he hastened across the Tay to the town of Dundee, where he halted for a night or two.

Amongst the officers of the Scotch dragoons there were some who had not forgotten their old chief, and who were ready to avail themselves of any favourable opportunity that occurred to join themselves to him. One of them was William Livingstone, a relative of the Colonel's. Captain Creichton, who had served with Claverhouse in the west, was another. It was arranged between them to enter into communication with Lady Dundee; and it was Creichton who undertook to act as messenger. Making his way to Dudhope privately and by night, he assured the Viscountess that the regiment in which he served would be at her husband's command, as soon as he pleased to give the word. This acceptable news was dispatched north. Creichton, who did not belong to either of the two troops that were left in Dundee, but had been obliged to follow Mackay into the Highlands, received a reply to the effect that Dundee had written to James to send him two thousand foot and one thousand horse out of Ireland, and that, as soon as those forces had arrived, he would expect his friends to join him with the dragoons.

In the hope of securing this important and welcome reinforcement, he resolved to make his way south, towards Dundee, where a part of the regiment was stationed. An intercepted despatch from Mackay to the Master of Forbes having given him some information as to the plan by which it was intended to check his movements, he waited at the Cairn-o'-Mount till the General was within eight miles of him, near Fettercairn. Understanding that it would be unsafe to advance further, in view of the dispositions that had been taken to surround him, he turned back again to Castle Gordon, where the Earl of Dunfermline joined him with forty or fifty gentlemen.

It appears to have been from Castle Gordon that Dundee dispatched a messenger to Lochiel to inform him of the situation. After consultation amongst the neighbouring Highland chiefs, it was decided that a detachment of eight hundred men, under Macdonald of Keppoch, should be sent to escort him into Lochaber. But Keppoch, whom the poetical chronicler describes as a man whom love of plunder would impel to any crime, had his own ends to serve. He was at feud with the Macintosh, and the town of Inverness had taken sides with the Macintosh. Instead of marching to meet Dundee, he led his forces against the town, from the magistrates of which he extorted the promise of a ransom of four thousand merks. The hasty arrival of Dundee, to whom information of Keppoch's outrageous conduct had been conveyed, put an end to this state of siege. But the weakness of his following obliged him to adopt a conciliatory policy towards the freebooter. He assured the magistrates, who appealed to him, that Keppoch had no warrant from him to be in arms, much less to plunder. Beyond that, however, he could only give his bond that, at the King's return, the money exacted by Keppoch should be made good. Having so far humoured the plundering laird, Dundee depended on his help to engage Mackay. But Keppoch, to whom honour and glory meant little, and for whom booty was everything, found various reasons for refusing his co-operation ; whilst his followers declared that they could do nothing without the consent of their master. Their object was, in reality, to add to their spoil, by harrying the country, and to retire with it to their mountain fastnesses.

Dundee was sorely disappointed at this untoward incident. So fully did he expect to be joined by Keppoch's men that he had already written to the magistrates of Elgin to prepare quarters for nine hundred or a thousand Highlanders besides his own cavalry. And now, instead of turning round on his pursuer, he was obliged to make his way through Stratherrick to Invergarry and Kilcummin, and thence into the wilds of Badenoch. Throughout this march, Dundee did not relax his efforts to enlist recruits, and he succeeded in engaging the greater part of the men of note to be ready at call to join in his master's service. Feeling that he might now depend on the active co-operation of the Highland chiefs, about the sixth or seventh of May, from the isolated farm of Presmukerach, in a secluded district between Cluny and Dalwhinnie, he issued a royal letter, calling upon the clans to meet him in Lochaber on the eighteenth of the month.

In the meantime, however, it was not Dundee's intention to remain idle. On the 9th of May, he was at Blair. Thence he advanced next day to Dunkeld, where, coming unexpectedly upon an agent of the new Government, who, with the help of the military, had been gathering the revenues of the district, he relieved him of the money, and

secured the arms of his escort.   This was but an incident.
The real object of the raid was seventeen miles further.
Dundee had received information that William Blair of
Blair, and his lieutenant Pollock were raising a troop in
the county of Perth, for the new Government; and he
had resolved to interfere with their recruiting.   Leaving
Dunkeld in the middle of the night, he was at Perth by
two o'clock in the morning, with seventy followers.   No
attack was expected, and no resistance was offered.   Blair
and Pollock were taken prisoners in their beds; and
several officers of the new levies were also captured.
Secure from surprise, the invading troopers carried out
their work deliberately and thoroughly; and when they
retired, about eleven o'clock next morning, the spoil they
took with them included arms, gunpowder, public-money,
and forty horses.   It is said that, on being brought before
Dundee, Blair had protested with some indignation against
the treatment to which he had been subjected, and that
the Viscount had curtly replied, 'You take prisoners for
the Prince of Orange, and we take prisoners for King
James, and there's an end of it.'

From Perth, Dundee retired to Scone, where an unwilling host, the Viscount of Stormont, was obliged to
accord him the hospitality of a dinner.   Knowing what
pains and penalties were incurred by holding intercourse
with one who had been outlawed as a traitor and a rebel,
Stormont lost no time in informing the President of the
Convention of the untoward incident.   But although he
urged the excuses that the dinner had been forced from
him, and that his 'intercommuning' had been wholly
involuntary, the Committee was not satisfied.   Stormont,
together with his uncle and his father-in-law, who happened
to be staying with him at the time, was subsequently
put to considerable trouble for the delinquency of having
been compelled to entertain the unbidden and unwelcome
guest.

Dundee had not forgotten the errand on which he had
originally started from the north, but which Mackay's
advance had obliged him to abandon for a time.   By way

of Cargill, Cupar-Augus, and Meigle, he worked his way round to Glamis, within less than twenty miles of Dundee. He utilised the circuitous march by detaching some of his troopers to collect revenues, in the name of the King, from the neighbouring villages; and not less acceptable than the money thus brought in, was the accession of half a score of volunteers amongst whom were Hallyburton, Fullerton, and a third whose is variously given as Venton, Fenton, and Renton. But even with these added to it, the little force with which he re-entered Glen Ogilvy did not amount to more than eighty.

In the afternoon of the 13th of May, the inhabitants of Dundee were startled by the alarming intelligence that an armed force was advancing over the Seidlaws to attack them. Hardly had they completed a rough and hasty preparation for defence by barring the gates and barricading the streets, when the redoubted leader appeared on the summit of the Law, of which his troopers held the base and the declivities. What the scared citizens took for a serious attack was merely a demonstration, devised for the purpose of affording the friendly dragoons an opportunity of effecting a junction with Dundee. William Livingstone appears to have understood the hint; for, according to the poetical chronicle of James Philip of Almerieclose, he endeavoured to head a feigned sortie at the head of the dragoons and of three hundred citizens whom he had enlisted for the Jacobite cause. But, by some means, of which there is no record, Captain Balfour, who was a staunch partisan of the new Government, succeeded in frustrating the attempt.

At nightfall Dundee retired to Glen Ogilvy, without the reinforcement which he had hoped to secure. All that he was able to take back with him as the result of his raid consisted in three hundred pounds of cess and excise, which he succeeded in seizing, and the baggage of a camp which lay outside the town, and which had been hastily abandoned at his approach. By the other side, this demonstration was looked upon as a daring attack. In the excitement which the news of it caused on reaching Edinburgh, the Convention gave orders that six firkins of powder should be sent from Bo'ness to Dundee, and that Hastings's infantry, and Berkley's horse should reinforce the garrison. Urgent despatches were also forwarded to Mackay, in Inverness, and brought less welcome than trustworthy information as to the movements of the man in pursuit of whom he was supposed to be.

IX

THE HIGHLAND CAMPAIGN

THE date fixed for the meeting of the clans was drawing near ; and, after a brief rest, Dundee was again in the saddle. By way of Cupar, Dunkeld, Comrie, and Garth, he shaped his course to Loch Rannoch, and thence over the Grampians, through wild and rugged paths, to Loch Treig and Lochaber. There he was received with all honour and respect by Sir Ewen Cameron of Lochiel, who assigned to his use a house at a little distance from his own, and supplied him with such conveniences as the country afforded. The chief of the Camerons was the most remarkable Highland figure of the time. He had always shown himself a staunch adherent of the Stuart cause, and his veneration for the memory of its great champion, Montrose, was proverbial amongst his kinsmen and friends. His own loyalty was above temptation ; and when, at the suggestion of Mackenzie of Tarbat, Mackay made an attempt to bribe him into submission to the new Government, the letters containing the proffered terms, were contemptuously left unanswered. It was mainly through the influence of Lochiel that the coalition of the clans had been effected. He himself brought to the royal cause a contingent of a thousand men, whom he had never led but to victory.

In accordance with the old Highland custom, Dundee sent round the fiery cross, immediately on his arrival in Lochaber. During the week which would have to elapse before the chieftains could all bring their followers to the trysting-place, he utilised his enforced leisure by drilling his small body of cavalry, and accustoming the horses to stand fire. The time at his disposal was insufficient to allow of his putting the infantry through a course of military training, and, on the advice of Lochiel he refrained from interfering with the rude but effective tactics of the Highlanders.

At length, about the 25th of May, the gathering of the clans was complete, and Dundee held a review of his army in the plain of Macomer. There was the brave Glengarry with three hundred warriors in the flower of vigorous manhood ; and following him closely was his brother with a hundred more. Next came Glencoe, huge-limbed, but strong and active, accompanied by another hundred claymores. Macdonald of Sleat headed a body of five hundred clansmen from the Isles of which he was the Lord. The men of Uist, of Knoydart, and of Moydart, marched under the leadership of their youthful chief, Allan Macdonald, Captain of Clan Ranald ; and two hundred men, as wild as himself were gathered about Keppoch, the notorious raider, the 'Colonel of the Cows,' as he was dubbed by Dundee, because of his particular skill in finding out cattle, when they were driven to the hills, to be out of his way.

All these, some fifteen hundred in the aggregate, belonged to the great clan Donald. They were all armed alike, and carried into battle, as their emblem, a bunch of wild heather, hung from the point of a spear. Under Dundee, the Macdonalds formed one battalion of twenty companies. The thousand men that composed the Cameron contingent doubtless included the various septs of the great clan, as well as some of the proscribed and scattered Macgregors, between whom and the Camerons there existed a close friendship.

From the various branches of the Macleans, another thousand men gathered around the blue standard of the tribe. The two hundred retainers of Stewart of Appin, together with those of Macneill of Barra, of Macleod of Raasay, of Fraser of Payers, of Fraser of Culduthill, of Grant of Urquhart, of Macnaughten, Macallister, Maclaughlane, and Lamont, helped to swell the ranks of Dundee's infantry, and to bring up its numbers to a total, which, if the enumeration of one who was present, and bore the leader's standard, be not grossly exaggerated, must have amounted to close on four thousand. Dundee's own following consisted of some eighty horse, composed of his veteran troopers, reinforced by a few noblemen and gentlemen. The most notable of these were the Earl of Dunfermline, Lord Dunkeld, Sir Alexander Innes, Edmonstone of Newton, Clelland of Faskin, the three recruits who had joined Dundee after the raid on Perth, a Bruce, who may have been Captain Bruce of Earlshall, Graham of Duntroone, and David Graham, the leader's own brother.

On the same day, after a stirring address from Dundee, who promised them that they should see him in the van whenever he hurled their united bands against the foe, the Highlanders marched forth towards Glen Spey. Glengarry, accompanied by thirty horse, opened the march. The rear was brought up by Fayers with his marshalled clan. By the evening of the 28th of May, Dundee had pitched his camp near the Castle of Raits, a few miles from Kingussie.

The 29th of May was a date which the adherents of the Stuarts held in special reverence. It was that of the birth of Charles II., and it was also that of his entry into London, at the Restoration. A day marked by two such events was considered specially auspicious; and its annual recurrence was hailed by commemorative celebrations. It offered an opportunity for a general and public expression of loyalty to the cause, which Dundee did not neglect; and with impressive ceremony he himself lighted a huge bonfire in the middle of the camp, and drank to the memory of the late King, and the success of his brother.

But the day was to be kept in a more practical way. Within accessible distance lay the Castle of Ruthven. In it Mackay had placed a garrison under Captain John Forbes, for the purpose of facilitating communication with Ramsay, who was expected with reinforcements from the south. Dundee opened hostilities by sending a force under Keppoch to demand the surrender of the Castle. Forbes returned a spirited answer to the summons, and made a brave show of resistance; but perceiving how futile it would be, in view of the preparations which were being made for the assault, he came to terms, and promised to lay down his arms, if, within three days, Mackay did not come to his relief.   But the General remained at Alvie, to which he had advanced from Inverness, and the Castle was evacuated at the expiration of the delay agreed upon.

Forbes was treated with remarkable consideration by Dundee.   He was allowed to pass through the camp with his garrison; and having noticed that the horses were all saddled and bridled, he concluded that immediate action was intended, and reported accordingly when he reached Mackay.   On his way to join his chief, he met two of his troopers making for Dundee's camp.   They alleged that they had been sent out to reconnoitre; and though warned of the danger which they ran of being captured, they pursued their way towards Raits.   This circumstance having also been communicated to Mackay, he opened an inquiry from which it resulted that the troopers were messengers who had been sent to arrange for the desertion of the Scots dragoons.   By the measures which the General at once adopted, the plan was again frustrated.

In the meantime, Dundee, whom rumours of an intended attack had reached, sent Bruce with a dozen troopers to ascertain their truth.   He returned with the information that Mackay was encamped near Alvie, and did not appear to have made any preparations for an advance.   At this, Dundee himself determined to move forward.   As he was pressing towards Alvie, he was startled to see that the Castle of Dunachton which he had passed shortly before, and left unharmed, was in a blaze.   The marauding Keppoch had again been at work.   After setting fire to Ruthven, as he had been ordered to do, he had further gratified his own love of plunder and of revenge by pillaging and destroying the old castle of his enemy the Mackintosh.

If discipline was to be maintained, Dundee could not tolerate such conduct, even on the part of so powerful a chieftain as Keppoch, and he sharply called the offender to task for it.   He told him in presence of all the officers of his small army, that 'he would much rather choose to serve as a common soldier amongst disciplined troops, than command such men as he, who seemed to make it his business to draw the odium of the country upon him.' Keppoch, whom no man had probably overawed before, muttered an excuse, and promised to abide strictly by the commander's orders for the future.

On reaching Alvie, Dundee discovered that Mackay had broken up his camp and was in full retreat. For four days he followed him so persistently and so closely that, on one occasion parties of his Highlanders were within shot of the rear-guard. If night had not come on, nothing, in all probability, could have saved the retreating troops. But the ground was dangerous, the march had been long, and the open country of Strathbogie, now only three miles distant, would have given Mackay's cavalry too much advantage over their pursuers. Dundee ordered a halt.

Next morning, having learnt that Mackay had marched ten miles further, he lay still all day. This was on the 5th of June. That same day, he received information that Barclay and Lesly's regiments, from Forfar and Cupar-Angus, had joined Mackay at Suy Hill. His old friends in the Scotch dragoons, who had dispatched the messenger with these tidings, communicated the further intelligence, that the Duke of Berwick was reported to have been captured, and that a party which had endeavoured to effect a landing in Scotland was also said to have been beaten back. They told him, too, that they were now surrounded by English horse and dragoons themselves, and that, in spite of their desire to cast in their lot with his, they could not avoid fighting against him, if there were an engagement. Under these circumstances, they begged him to go out of the way for a time, until better news should come.

The advice was judicious. Dundee adopted it, and turned back towards Badenoch. His action was fully justified by the event. With the reinforcements which he had received from the south, Mackay at once turned back upon his pursuer, whom he hoped to take by surprise. But his night march was in vain. When he reached

Edinglassie, where the Highland camp had been, it **was** only to find that Dundee was already on his way to Cromdale. He sent a party of horse in pursuit; but the troopers never came within sight of the rear-guard, though they succeeded in cutting off some of the plundering stragglers.

During this retreat, there occurred an incident which helped to cheer Dundee; for it was not with a glad heart that he had turned away from the enemy, and, to add to the disappointment which he felt, he was so prostrate through illness, at this critical moment, that his rate of progress had to be reduced to a few miles a day—to less than six miles in all on the 7th and 8th of June. On the 9th of June, whilst Dundee, who had moved up the Spey, was in the neighbourhood of Abernethy, Mackay gave orders to Sir Thomas Livingstone to cross the river with a detachment of dragoons, for the purpose of supporting the Laird of Grant's men, who had been hard pressed by parties of the Highlanders. Whilst on this mission, an advance guard of the troopers fell in with a body of three hundred Macleans, who, under Lochbery, were on their way to join Dundee. In the engagement that followed, the cavalry was completely routed, and the clansmen, elated with victory and laden with spoil stripped from the slain were enthusiastically welcomed in Dundee's camp.

It had been Dundee's intention to take up a strong position in Rannoch, but, as he wrote in one of his despatches, finding that the Lochaber men were going away every night by forties and fifties, with droves of cattle, and that all the rest, who were laden with plunder of Grant's land and others, were equally anxious to return home with it, he yielded to necessity, came into Lochaber with them, and dismissed them to their respective houses, with injunctions to be ready within a few days, if the enemy pursued. If he did not, they were to lay still till further orders. Mackay, on his side, seeing that Dundee had reached a district where there were no good roads, and where it would be impossible to buy the provisions without which no regular body of forces could subsist together, also resolved to retire from the field for a time. In a despatch forwarded to

Ireland through Hay, the position at this time was described as follows : ' My Lord Dundee hath continued in Lochaber, guarded only by two hundred, commanded by Sir Alexander Maclean. But, being in the heart of Glengarry and Lochiel's lands, he thinks himself secure enough ; though he had not, as he has, the Captam of Clanranald, with six hundred men within ten miles of him, and Maclean, Sir Donald, and Macleod marching towards him. So that he can march with near four thousand ; or refresh in safety, till such time as the state of affairs of Ireland may allow the King to send forces to his relief : which if it please God shall fall out, there is all appearance of forming a considerable army, notwithstanding that the people are a little disheartened by the unexpected surrender of the Castle of Edinburgh, which, as said, was only by despair the Duke had of any relief, though he wanted not from my Lord Dundee, by a third hand, all the encouragement he could give.' This brings the Highland campaign forward to about the middle of June.

In spite of the circumstances which had made it necessary for him to retire to Lochaber, Dundee entertained no doubt as to the ultimate success of the cause which he championed. Though indecisive, the result of his military operations was such as to inspire him with confidence in himself, and in the fighting powers, if not in the discipline, of his Highlanders. With them, he had more than held his own under difficulties that might well have discouraged a less energetic and resourceful leader. He had been obliged to begin the campaign with but fifty pounds of powder, for all the great towns and sea-ports were hostile to him, and would sell none. He had no money, and could raise none on his own credit ; and, worse than all, the help on which he depended, and on the promise of which he had induced the chieftains to join him, had not come. Yet, in spite of all this, he had suffered no reverse ; and though the bulk of his army was disbanded, he knew that a few days would suffice to bring the clans about him again, in all their former strength, and with more than their former devotion.

For he had won their respect by his own cheerful endurance of all the hardships of the campaign, and their affection by the sympathy and the ready help which he had given them to bear their share.

Of that which might, indeed, have discouraged him, of the true state of affairs outside Scotland, he knew nothing. He had not only been kept in ignorance, he appears to have been systematically deceived. As late as the 23rd of June, writing to Macleod of Macleod to communicate to him the news he had just received, he gave him a glowing account of what was being achieved in Ireland. Hay, who had himself been at the siege of Londonderry, had just reported, that more than three weeks before, the inhabitants were reduced to such extremities that horse flesh was sold for sixpence a pound, that, for cannon-balls they were shooting lumps of brick wrapped in pewter plates, that an attempt at relief had been defeated with great loss. Fifty-two sail of French warships were already in Ireland; eighty more were on their way from Brest; some of the French fleet had been seen amongst the islands, and had taken the two Glasgow frigates; Edinburgh had lost heart, and offered to surrender if King James would grant terms; in short, everything was so hopeful and so far advanced, that if Macleod did not hasten to land his men, he would have but little occasion to do the King much service.

In view of such hopeful accounts, Dundee who could have no means of testing their truth, and who had no suspicion of their exaggeration, might well feel confident of success, if only, as had repeatedly been promised, King James would send him the reinforcements and the supplies so anxiously expected, 'ammunition, and three or four thousand arms of different sorts, some horse, some foot.' Even when he learnt, about the middle of July, that the only succour to be got from Ireland, consisted of three hundred ill-trained men, with whom Cannon had effected a landing at Inverlochy, he did not lose confidence, and an attempt to bring him to terms, of which his brother-in-law, Lord Strathnaver was the intermediary, was met with a dignified refusal. Nor did his enemies themselves seem to think that his power and influence had yet begun to wane ; for they thought it worth their while to set a price of twenty thousand pounds sterling on his head.

But a crisis was now at hand. About the middle of July, Lord John Murray, the Marquis of Athole's eldest son, in accordance with an agreement come to with Mackay, had gone into the Highlands, for the purpose of raising a body of his father's followers. He knew their loyalty to the Stuart cause, and had no hope of being able to induce them to take sides for the new Government. But he might devise means to keep them neutral; and no more was required of him. 'Keep the Athole men from joining Dundee,' Mackay had said to him, 'and that is all I ask, or can expect, from your father's son.' He succeeded in bringing together twelve hundred men, with whom he intended to garrison the important Castle of Blair.

Dundee had been duly informed of Murray's levies ; but he affected to believe in the young chief's loyalty, and wrote to him, from his quarters in Struan, on the other side of the Garry, suggesting that they should meet to concert what was fittest to be done for the good of the country, and the service of their lawful King. Receiving no answer to his letter, he gave orders to Stewart of Ballechin, a retainer of Athole's, and a staunch Jacobite, to occupy the Castle, in the name of King James. Two further communications to Murray having been similarly disregarded, Dundee dispatched two of his officers to him, with a final appeal. They were instructed to deliver it into Murray's own hands, and to receive his positive answer; but Murray declined to grant them an interview.

When this became known to the clansmen whom he had with him, and from whom he had so far succeeded in concealing his real designs, they called upon him to let them know what course of action he had resolved upon, and plainly told him that if he meant to join Dundee they would follow him, but that if he refused to do so, they would immediately forsake him. In vain he attempted

to threaten them into submission. They were true to
their word. Filling their bonnets with water, they drank
the King's health, and turned their backs on the chief
who had thought to make them traitors, against their will,
to the cause of the Stuarts.

In the meantime, Dundee had been active in other
directions. His summons to the clans had again been
sent forth, and orders given for a general meeting at Blair,
where he himself arrived, at latest, on the 26th of July.
That same day Mackay marched from Perth to Dunkeld,
with about four thousand foot, and two troops of horse
and dragoons.

There still remained two days to the date fixed for the
gathering of the claymores, when Dundee moved from the
camp at Blair to meet Mackay's advance. He could not
wait for the arrival of his full force; but he hoped that the
deficiency in numbers would be compensated by the mettle
and determination of those who had joined. To satisfy
himself that the martial ardour of the clans had not suffered
from the long years of inactivity which had elapsed since
last they met an enemy, at Philiphaugh, he put it to an
effective test. At early dawn, when the men were still
sleeping in their plaids, in the heather, he caused the
alarm to be sounded. In an instant, every man had
sprung to his feet, and seizing his arms had run to take
up his position in front of the camp. When the Viscount
perceived this, says one of the chroniclers who record the
incident, and that not a man of them retired, with full
assurance, he instantly began his march to meet the enemy.

Before deciding to leave Blair, Dundee had called
together a council of war composed of all the leading
men who had joined him. The question to be discussed
was, whether it was wiser to remain encamped until the
arrival of all the Highland contingents, or to march
forward at once to meet Mackay. The old officers, who
were accustomed to the command of regular troops,
favoured the former alternative, and urged that it would
be imprudent to risk an engagement against an army
which exceeded theirs by more than half, and was com-

posed of trained soldiers, whilst their own forces consisted of raw, undisciplined men, who had never seen blood, whose strength was impaired by the sufferings and privations of a long march, and whose spirit was damped by disappointments.

Glengarry, on the other hand, represented that, although the clansmen's endurance had been taxed by want of provisions as well as by fatigue, they were but little affected by hardships to which their own way of living inured them; and that, in spite of what they had gone through, they were both able and ready to fight an equal number of the enemy's best troops, and had a fair chance of beating them. Still, even he did not recommend a general engagement before the arrival of the remaining claymores had brought their numbers more nearly to an equality with those of their opponents. His advice, which met with the approval of most of the chieftains, was that they should keep the army constantly in sight of the enemy, and should post their men on strong ground, where they would be safe from attack themselves, and whence they could easily sally forth, at every available opportunity, to harass the foe.

Alone of those present, Lochiel had refrained from giving any sign of adherence to the views of either party; and Dundee noticing this, called upon him, in terms most flattering to the old chief, to declare his opinion. It was given without hesitation: To fight the enemy. As he supported this advice by pointing to the eagerness of the men, and by enumerating the disadvantages of a delay, it was observed that Dundee's countenance brightened, and that he listened with obvious satisfaction to his spirited yet wise words. When his turn came to speak, he told the Council that his sentiments had just been expressed by one who added to them the weight of long experience and of intimate knowledge, and that his voice, like that of Lochiel, was for immediate and decisive action, a course which was consequently resolved upon.

Before the Council broke up, the venerable chieftain again rose to speak. He had promised, he said, and would yield implicit obedience to all Dundee's orders; but he requested that, before they separated, he might be allowed to give one command, not in his own name, but in that of the whole Council. It was the unanimous wish of all present that Dundee should not engage personally, for on him depended the fate, not only of their brave little army, but also of their king and of their country. 'If your Lordship deny us this reasonable demand,' he added, 'for my own part I declare that neither I, nor any I am concerned in, shall draw a sword on this important occasion, whatever construction shall be put on the matter.' In his reply to this appeal, Dundee admitted that, if he fell, his death might be a loss to them; but he reminded his hearers of the temper of their men. If the least reason were given them to doubt the personal courage of their leader, they would lose their respect for him, and give him, at best, but grudging obedience. For this reason, he begged to be permitted to give one 'shear-darg'—that is, one harvest day's work—to the King, his master, that he might have an opportunity of convincing the brave clans that he could hazard his life in that service, as freely as the meanest of them. If this were granted him he pledged his word never again to risk his person, so long as he had the honour of commanding them. Finding him inflexible in the chivalrous resolution which he had couched as a request, the Council reluctantly yielded.

On the morning of the 27th of July, Mackay left his quarters in Dunkeld. By ten o'clock he had reached the southern extremity of the Pass of Killiecrankie, where he halted for two hours. At noon he again gave the order to advance. The Pass into which he led his army consisted of an almost straight road, fully two miles in length, and so narrow that barely half a dozen men could march abreast. To the right it was flanked by lofty mountains. The precipitous banks of the Garry skirted it on the left; and, on the other side of the river, a thickly wooded mountain hemmed in the landscape. Through this wild and rugged defile Balfour, Ramsay and Kenmore opened the march with their three battalions. Then came Belhaven's troop of horse, followed by Leven's regiment, and a battalion of the General's.   Over twelve hundred baggage horses formed a long line behind them, protected by a rear-guard which consisted of the Earl of Annandale's troop of horse and Hastings's regiment.

Impressed by the wildness of the surroundings, and conscious of the danger to which it would be exposed in the event of an attack, the army moved cautiously but cumbrously on.   As it advanced without discovering any sign of the presence of the enemy, his neglect to avail himself of the obvious advantages which the nature of the ground offered him, inspired a new fear.   Some carefully prepared trap at the further end seemed to afford the only intelligible explanation of his action in leaving the pass free.   Even Mackay himself did not realise that the only stratagem which Dundee had devised was an engagement that should not merely retard, but wholly scatter his opponent's forces.

At length, the open ground on the bank of the Garry was reached.   As his men debouched into it, Mackay drew them up three deep, without changing the relative position of the regiments.   The extreme left was thus held by Balfour.   Ramsay and Kenmore came next, and were posted between him and two troops of horse that occupied the centre.   Leven, Mackay and Hastings were on the right.   Some short, portable leather cannon, that could hardly be dignified with the name of artillery were placed behind the horse.   The whole line faced towards Blair, from which the enemy was expected to move forward. And, indeed, before long, the General perceived what he thought was the advance guard, coming down the valley towards him.   It was in reality but a small detachment that had been sent on for the purpose of attracting his attention.   Dundee, with his main body had wound his way round to the left, and his Highlanders were soon seen taking up their position on some elevated ground that commanded Mackay's right wing.   Without altering the disposition of his line of battle, the General wheeled it round to face the clansmen, a movement by which he put the river and the steep ridge above it immediately in his rear, and rendered his own position far more precarious in the event of a defeat, whilst the rise of the ground towards the hills in his front prevented him from attacking the enemy except under obviously disadvantageous conditions.

In the meantime, Dundee was making his own dispositions for the coming fight. Acting under the advice of Lochiel, who knew the spirit of emulation by which the several clans were animated, he drew them up in such a way that each of them should have a regiment in Mackay's line assigned to it. The Macleans, under their youthful chief, were posted on the extreme right. The Irish contingent, commanded by Colonel Pearson occupied the next position, and had the Tutor of Clanranald with his battalion on their immediate left. A fourth battalion, composed of the men whom the stalwart Glengarry led to battle, made up the right wing. The left consisted of two others, of which Lochiel's was one, and Sir Donald Macdonald's the other. The only cavalry at Dundee's disposal consisted of a few Lowland gentlemen and some remains of his old troop, not exceeding forty horse in all, and these 'very lean and ill-kept.' It was posted in the centre, to face Mackay's hundred sabres. It should have been under the orders of the Earl of Dunfermline; but that very morning, Sir William Wallace, a gentleman who had come over from Ireland, produced a commission which appointed him to the command hitherto held by the Earl. Though deeply mortified Dunfermline had submitted without demur to the unjust and ill-advised supersession, for which Melfort, Wallace's brother-in-law, was probably responsible. His loyalty to the cause which he served prevented him from raising a dispute at so critical a time.

For two hours the armies stood facing each other, within musket-shot, without engaging, though some desultory skirmishing appears to have been going on towards the left, between some Macleans and the regiment opposed to them, whilst the guns in Mackay's centre kept up an intermittent and harmless fire. During this long pause before the battle both leaders addressed their troop. In spite of his superiority in numbers, Mackay did not hide from his men that the task before them was no easy one. In encouraging them to it, he pointed out that, in such a place and with such foemen, they could not hope for safety in flight, but must win it for themselves by the defeat of the enemy. His words were greeted with a cheer, which to Lochiel who heard it, seemed wanting in enthusiasm, and from which he drew for his own followers an omen of victory.

In Dundee's allocution there was a spirited appeal to the loyalty and patriotism of the clansmen. He urged them to behave like true Scotsmen, in defence of their King, their Religion, and their Country. He asked nothing of them but what they should see him do before them. For those who fell, there would be the comfort and the honour of having died in the performance of their duty, and as became true men of valour and of conscience; and to those who lived and won the battle, he promised a reward of a gracious King, and the praise of all good men.

It was not till eight o'clock on that summer evening that Dundee gave orders for the advance of his two thousand men. Casting off brogues and plaids the clansmen moved forward down the slope. They were met with a heavy fire, which grew more terrible as they approached the treble line of their opponents. But with wonderful resolution they obeyed the orders given them, and reserved their own till they came to within a few yards of the enemy. Then they poured it in upon them 'like one great clap of thunder,' and, throwing away their muskets, fell upon the infantry with their claymores before it had time to fix bayonets to receive them. 'After that,' in the words of Lochiel's 'Memoirs,' 'the noise seemed hushed; and the firing ceasing on both sides, nothing was heard for some few moments but the sullen and hollow clashes of the broadswords, with the dismal groans and cries of dying and wounded men.'

Dundee, who had joined his small body of horse, ordered Wallace to attack the troopers whilst the clans were scattering the infantry, and himself rode forward to take part in the charge. But Sir William, the nominal commander, 'not being too forward,' Dundee would have met with no support if the Earl of Dunfermline, taking in the situation at a glance, had not dashed forward, with some sixteen volunteers who left the laggard ranks. Mackay's troopers did not stop to receive the shock of this handful of men, but joined the infantry in their flight. Nor did the gunners make a better stand; and their clumsy ordnance was captured before Wallace came up. Then Dundee, wheeling to the enemy's right, charged Mackay's own regiment, which, after delivering a last volley, turned and fled like the rest, in spite of the General's efforts to rally it.

Pausing for a moment to look round the field, the victorious leader perceived that Sir Donald Macdonald's battalion, 'which had not shown so great resolution as the rest of the Highlanders,' was hesitating in its attack upon Hastings's regiment. He was on his way to urge it forward, when a shot struck him in the side and inflicted a mortal wound. He reeled in the saddle, and was falling from his horse; but one of his officers, named Johnstone, was at hand to catch him in his arms and to help him to the ground. As he lay there, the dying leader asked how the day went. 'The day goes well for the King,' replied Johnstone, 'but I am sorry for your Lordship.' But Dundee felt the comfort which he had so shortly before promised those who should fall; 'it is the less matter for me,' he said, 'seeing the day goes well for my master.'

Besides Dundee himself, there lay on the fateful field some nine hundred men of his little army of hardly more than two thousand. Whether he died on the scene of his dearly-bought victory, or whether he was removed from it and survived long enough to dictate the letter which his Jacobite admirers have regarded as a last tribute of loyalty to his King, and his Whig opponents denounced as an unscrupulous forgery, are questions upon which too little depends to justify a discussion of them. He was buried at Blair.

INDEX

Lightning Source UK Ltd.
Milton Keynes UK
UKHW011212051118
331792UK00006B/698/P